M000306608

JAGUAR 'E' TYPE RESTORATION

Published by
KELSEY PUBLISHING LTD

Printed in Singapore by Stamford Press Pte Ltd
On behalf of Kelsey Publishing Ltd
Cudham Tithe Barn, Berrys Hill
Cudham, Kent, TN16 3AG
Tel: 01959 541444   Fax: 01959 541400

ISBN 1 873098 52 9

Acknowledgements
Our thanks go to Jim Patten for covering the 'Series 1' project.
Appreciation also to Nigel Thorley of the JAGUAR ENTHUSIASTS' CLUB for allowing
us to use their material on the 'Series III' for this book

CONTENTS

INTRODUCTION

Since its launch in 1961 the Jaguar E-Type has been top of the 'wish list' for many a sports car lover. Nearly forty years on, enthusiasm for this icon of motoring history seems undiminished.

Quite naturally therefore, both *Jaguar World* magazine and the Jaguar Enthusiasts' Club magazine, Jaguar Enthusiast, have featured restoration projects within their pages. In this, the latest book from Kelsey Publishing, the two projects have been brought together to form a comprehensive guide for the amateur.

Jim Patten, the well known motoring journalist and self confessed Jaguar fanatic, puts together the story of the restoration of his own 'Series 1' roadster by Henry Pearman of 'Eagle 'E' types'. While the human Jaguar encyclopaedia Nigel Thorley, editor of *Jaguar Enthusiast*, writes of the work carried out by Dave Marks on the JDHT Series 3 V12 fixedhead.

Since the restoration of the 'Patten' roadster, it has been well used, and indeed, I have fond memories of the car framed in my rear view mirror, as we travelled in convoy from Lille to Arras on the E's first outing to France. Completion of the Series 3 V12 saw its return to the Jaguar Daimler Heritage Trust, where it forms part of the Trust's valuable collection of historic cars.

I am sure this book, with its informative text and numerous colour illustrations, will become a must for anyone contemplating work on their E-Type, from minor mechanical repairs to a full restoration.

As delivered to Henry Pearman for the first stage. With the bonnet off and front wheels off, a few of us wheeled it around like a wheelbarrow. Mileage is now 57,000.

PROJECT 'E' TYPE

Finally, after years of surreptitious looking for the right car, Jim Patten returns to the 'E' type fold.

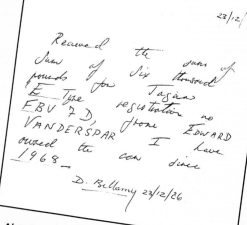

23/12/86

Sorry, dear, the new dining room suite will have to wait." How can I explain that with just two weeks before moving from Hornchurch to White Notley (where?), I am buying an 'E' type? I wasn't exactly looking for one, although my ear was maintained close to the ground just in case; it was simply that I can resist everything except temptation, as they say

The offer came by an unlikely route. Those who read every word of *Jaguar World* (like you do, of course) will remember that I defected for a while to a BMW CSL. Most of its parts came from Kent BMW specialist Munich Legends and it was through them that I eventually sold the car. One of their customers, Edward Vanderspaar, had fully-restored his CSL and casually mentioned that he would like to find a good home for his 'E' type. To cut

a long story not so long, we were introduced, I told him what I could afford (not very much), he told me what he wanted (a lot more), we got along famously and eventually had a deal. Her name is Jasmine.

Less about the whys, more about the car. Basic facts are: 4.2 'E' type roadster, date of manufacture September 6 1966, chassis number 1E1662, engine number 7E10102-9, colour dark blue with grey trim and blue hood. Options fitted: steering column lock and hard top.

This car is one of 9,548 4.2 open two-seaters with closed headlights, of the sort we now refer to as 'Series 1' 4.2 'E' types, produced between March 1964 and 1967/68. Of these only 1,182 were right-hand-drive, not all of which stayed in the UK of course as some were exported to

Above:
'Just Married'. 1988:
Edward Vanderspaar and his new bride Michelle set off in the 'E' type exactly two years from the day of purchase.

Below:
All part of the story: receipt from David Bellamy on the sale to Edward Vaderspar.

Australia and New Zealand for example.

Jaguar supplied this car through Astons at Preston to an Angus Boncroft of the same area. In 1968 ownership passed to David Bellamy (no, there is more than one) in west London.

Sometime in 1970 a drive shaft U/J failed and the car came off the road for, it was thought, just a little while. Then came a fuel crisis when it was not 'done' to be seen in gas-guzzlers. Petrol prices went through the roof and even cleared £1 a gallon (well, the pound was worth a bit more then). By the time normal service was resumed Mr Bellamy had developed a heart condition but still intended to have the minor job fixed and return the car to the road. Then, in the winter of 1986, he decided that this would never happen and so looked for a sympathetic new owner. With the various adverts set to appear in the right places, he conducted what could only be described as a series of interviews with applicants, most, it must be said, from the trade.

Edward Vanderspaar plays viola professionally. As Mr Bellamy's home was not too far from the BBC where Edward was playing, he found it convenient to attend the preliminary round of interviews. His genuine enthusiasm showed and he found success at the final meeting on December 23. The mileage at that point was around 49,000.

Somehow during its four years on the road the 'E' type had suffered more than its share of small dents, specifically on the driver's door, bonnet underpan and off-side rear wing. Despite this the car was incredibly sound. Edward had the car trailed home and carried out the necessary repairs to the drive shaft but, due to pressure of work, used a local Jaguar man to carry out the preparatory work prior to putting the 'E' type back on the road. There are 31 sheets of notes detailing the thoroughness with which this was done, checking that all valves moved and that the valve buckets rotated and so on. Subsequent work took the tally of notes to 53... Nothing major though, just good solid maintenance.

Then came the battle with the DVLC to retain the registration number. Edward had decided to obtain road tax on the original number and battle it out with the authorities. He won, backed with vehicle details from Jaguar and a letter from John Burton of the JDC's 'E' type Register.

Two years to the day of purchasing the 'E' type, Edward married Michelle. Almost a fairy tale, he had known her since he

Although this looks awful there is no rust here, just dents.

There's rust elsewhere, though. The nearside sill appears to be the worse although the floor looks good. We'll know more once we remove the outer sill.

was 11 and, at the allotted time, whisked her off to their wedding in Devon in the 'E' type. "Time was running a little short," said Edward, "and my best man in his XR3i had a devil of a job keeping up with the 'E' and I'm not a fast driver - he is."

Then came an audition for the New York Philharmonic Orchestra and, looking for peace and a bit of tranquillity, they took the 'E' type and viola to an old farmhouse (circa 10th century) in France and spent an idyllic month there. Michelle was once terrified when Edward had left the car for a short time while she was still in it. A small gang of Frenchmen surrounded the Jaguar and one got in the driver's side. He apologised profusely but said that his impulsive emotions had got the better of him. Then he left with no damage caused. A second European trip was taken the following year to Alsace. Michelle always kept a record of the trips and did not have to record any disasters although an alternator did fail on the

return from France.

Now as a senior member (well, not so senior, he's younger than me!) of the London Symphony Orchestra with a growing family, Edward found it difficult to justify keeping the 'E' type, particularly as it now needs to be looked at further. Alex Elliot, a BMW specialist, looks after Edward's BMW and in turn started work on the 'E' type. A seized caliper and oil seeping from the rear crankshaft seal started what would become a lengthy job. When I came in on the scene the engine was out, stripped and machined and the front suspension rebuilt. Alex was about to move into bigger premises and so really it was all change.

I have a lot of serious thinking to do now. This is not a car for a full nut and bolt restoration but equally it does need work, notably a pair of sills at the very least. I trailered the car down to Henry Pearman (Tel: 0825 830966), well-known 'E' type specialist, for the first stage of the

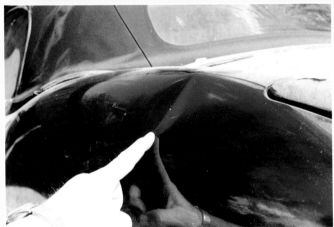

These are the sort of dents we will have to deal with. Nothing a good panel man can't handle.

More dents. The nose of the bonnet appears to have had a bad time but its structure, including the rust-vunerable seams, is very well-preserved.

resuscitation - bodywork repairs.

I am a little worried about hacking the sills off and losing the car's shape. Henry always works from a jig and, although that does mean removing the front frames and rear suspension, at least I know that none of the rigidity will be lost. As we looked over the car our excitement grew as Henry confirmed that of the 250 or so 'E' types that have been through their workshops, this was one of the very best right-hand-drive 'tubs' he had seen. Even the original tool kit is complete.

In an effort to retain the 'E' type's integrity, I will have as many original panels repaired as possible and, at this stage, that includes the bonnet. The sills have been ordered from Hutsons (Tel: 0274 669052) and we (by that I mean Henry Pearman and his team) shall begin work as soon as the jig is free. Join us over the coming months as we serialise the entire story, one of retention rather than replacement.

PROJECT E-TYPE

Jim Patten finds out exactly what he has bought as the 'E' type goes on the jig at Henry Pearman's Eagle 'E' types.

SPONSORED BY
DOUBLE 'S' EXHAUSTS LTD
STAINLESS STEEL

THE ORIGINAL AND FINEST STAINLESS STEEL EXHAUSTS

"They all look good until you open them up," was how Matt Dewhurst, Henry Pearman's body man, felt about 'E' types. He was a great calming influence, as I was getting a touch over-excited about the condition of the floors and bulkhead – panels that will rust at a drop of a hat. It was time to start the strip-down of the new project. We had concluded that at the very least a pair of sills with inner stiffeners would be needed. A little rust in the passenger door would need a repair but not a re-skin.

In an effort to keep the cost down, this impoverished scribe decided to do some of the donkey work. This suited Henry very well as, although the market is still not fully recovered, they are just about full to brimming with 'E' type restoration work, including JDU 877E, the factory road test car. The jig is rarely empty and I had to wait for a slot but at least that would give me time to strip the necessary parts. Pick-up points for the jig are the front frame mounts on the bulkhead and the rear axle mounts. The engine had already been removed and the bonnet was a loose fit so it was just a question of 'wheeling' the 'E' type in to the body shop. Left alone, with a pile of spanners, I set to, removing the front frames first. Servo, heater and all bits and pieces were soon packed into boxes with all nuts and bolts packed and labelled.

Now, I've removed my fair share of frames and had many a bolt shear so, when it came to the bottom bolts, I uttered a protecting chant, closed my eyes and went for it. Every bolt simply spun off without a hitch. I began to hope for good things. In no time the frames came away complete and, with Matt's help, we lifted

the assembly away. Next came the interior. The carpet floor mats had long since gone but the rest of the trim was not only complete, it was in astonishingly good condition – a little grubby from the years in storage but nothing that wouldn't respond to the right sort of treatment. Even the piping in the seats was intact.

It seemed as though every screw or nut that I touched relinquished its hold with just the right amount of resistance. It was particularly pleasing to find the sill covers peeling back without tearing or stretching, the first time these had been touched (as with most of the car) since 1966. When the seats came out, it became very clear that the floors and inner sills were exceptional, although we did (as Matt re-affirmed) expect to make some repairs to the inner sill.

Jaguar reckon 45 minutes to remove the rear suspension. It took me a little longer but not much. It was soon on the floor and the car ready to fit the jig. This is essentially a large, stiff girder base to which an 'E' type body fits to modified and stiffened front frames and a substantial

(continued)

With the 'E' type held firmly on the jig, the basic rigidity will remain no matter if some structural parts are removed.

The sill cover material came off with ease and is just as pliable as when new. With a bit of cleaning, it will be as good as new.

Eat your heart out 'E' type restorers – it's all Coventry steel in that floor pan. The front's the same too.

How many rear mounts still have their spacer shims intact? Those grubby mits belong to your esteemed scribe.

All lead must be melted away before starting work.

Removing the front frames was just a nut and bolt job. No rusty nuts, no disasters.

cradle at the rear. Any deficiency in the body alignment would show up now as the holes would not line up. True to form, FBV fitted perfectly.

Henry has had a few peculiar requests but to move the jig out to the courtyard of his farm for photographs was one of the strangest; the jig is not exactly mobile. We had great fun sorting out some wheels and hitching up the ageing Massey Ferguson tractor that Henry uses for moving immobile Jaguars.

Back in the bodyshop it was time for Matt to perform his craft. Using a torch, he burned away the lead at the front and rear bulkheads' panels. Then, using a spot weld drill, he gradually unpicked the sill, finally finishing with a cut through with an air chisel at the bulkhead panel and rear wing. Both floors were in perfect condition with each jacking point as good as in 1966

Of course Matt was absolutely correct; there was some rust on the inner sill but even he was surprised at how little. It was confined to a small area at the front of the inner sill. Absolutely zero in the rear wing and bulkhead panel. Although lightly rusted at the bottom, the inner sill stiffeners were removed after drilling out the spot welds. Matt pointed out a couple of areas where no spot welds had been

made, something alas, not uncommon. Maybe the lads at Jaguar were on piecework in the sixties and missing a handful of hidden welds speeded up their progress and subsequent earnings.

Alas, the sill front end closing panel had a tiny rust hole and we felt it would be madness not to replace it. It was removed at this stage but would not be replaced until the car was removed from the jig. After tidying up the edges, Matt used a grit recycling blaster to remove any surface rust. He decided to cut a much larger hole around the rusted area as he predicted that the surrounding metal would be a little on the thin side. The repair section that Matt made was flanged at the edges and this fitted exactly in the hole. By the time it was MIG-welded and ground back, the repair was as near to invisible mending as you could get.

Offering up the new sill, Matt gave me an option. To fit as Jaguar did would mean removing the outer bulkhead panel. The alternative would be to trim the sill and join it to the remains of the old sill, still welded under the panel. I opted for the latter as I was anxious to retain as many original parts as possible and didn't want to lose the bulkhead panel. Matt was particularly impressed by the sill supplied by Hutson as it had the right curves and

ran the full distance.

There's a great product on the market now, weld-through zinc primer. We used the 3M version. Before electrically welding any metal, the primer is sprayed on the mating surfaces. The weld passes through the primer without burning it away, leaving the metal fully protected. Matt uses a hole dinker to make a series of small holes along the edges of the replacement panels to get make sure that the MIG weld fully penetrates to the panel beneath. Both stiffeners were fitted (this time without missing any welds) in no time and then the sill was placed in position. Matt clipped and unclipped the grips holding the sill until he was absolutely sure of the position. Then he removed the door and took it to the bench for repair; he would need to know the position of this in relation to the sill before he was committed to welding.

How easy it looked when he measured and cut a couple of inches from the bottom of the door skin. And then, from a plain sheet of steel, he cut a section, rolled a flange edge and offered it to the door. After one or two adjustments he folded the edges, trimmed the corners and tucked the new piece into the original door skin. A trial fit of the door on the car confirmed the measurement and he

Once the sill has been cut away, the worst can be revealed – in this case, just that small hole on the lower right of the picture. Localised blasting cleans the metal of all rust.

Matt Dewhurst welds the inner sill repair from inside the car. Once finished and ground back, there is very little evidence of any welding.

Off come the bottom couple of inches of the door.

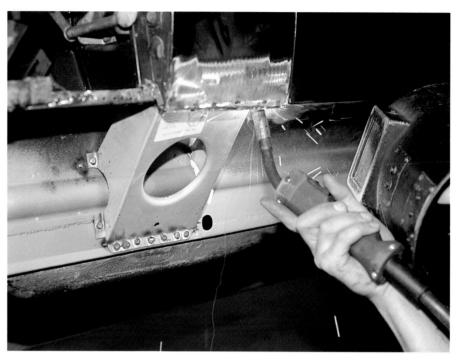

Inner sill stiffeners are welded in exactly the same location vacated by the originals. The product label can be removed with a thinners damped cloth.

Next a carefully-measured and cut strip of steel sheet is flanged as a repair panel.

Once the panel has been fitted, the door is offered to the car and then finally the edges are tapped fully home and the panel welded in place.

When the door and sill are in tune, the sill is welded along its edges. If you ever have trouble sleeping, try counting the number of spot welds on an 'E' type sill instead of sheep.

After the welds have been ground down, the panels can be lead loaded. The surface must be absolutely clean and Matt spends a lot of time over this using the blaster, rotary wire brush or any other medium that might serve. The metal is then heated, painted with solder-paint and heated again and wiped over with a clean cloth. This leaves a receptive surface for the lead. That in turn is not quite melted but heated until it takes a jelly like texture. Then it is applied to the work. When Matt does it, the lead stays put. When I try, there's more lead on the floor than the car.

returned it to the bench to be welded, without distortion. It was really impressive to watch and with such a casual air he might just as well have been making a cup of tea.

With the door back in place and all gaps right, Matt set about the final welding of the sill. Each little hole took a small MIG weld and was eventually ground back to give the impression of the original spot weld. The bulkhead join was a neat, continuous line that, when ground back, would be leaded. That operation was carried out with the same aplomb as all of the work so far.

On a lighter note, you will have noticed in the 'Original Mk 1' feature, a Jaguar-friendly boxer dog. Mike Hawthorn had one and Henry, too, keeps a boxer, Agip (yes, named after the Italian oil). Sadly we have lost ours. Gus had a cancer and died at the age of six but we will have another. Are there many more Jaguar owners with boxer dogs or is the connection purely coincidental?

In the next issue, the 'E' type is removed from the jig and the bodywork repairs continue.

Our thanks go to Henry Pearman, Eagle 'E' types (Tel: 0825 830966) for all their help and good nature during this feature. Panels were supplied by the Hutson Motor Company Ltd (Tel: 0274 669052).

PROJECT E-TYPE

Jim Patten embarks on a 'Save the Bonnet Campaign' at Henry Pearman's Eagle 'E' types.

I f you own a classic Jaguar like the 'E' type where there is an excellent spares back-up, it's so easy just to pop down the road and buy a new this or that – disregarding the expense, of course. But there is a great deal of satisfaction in giving new life to a genuine old part. Naturally there are times when there is no way out and a direct replacement is the only sensible (or safe) thing.

I see so many restorers now discarding 'E' type bonnets almost as a matter of course. New replacements (still made by the original manufacturers, Abbey Panels) can be obtained even today (although they happen to be on back order at the moment) and so it is almost regarded as a must. For most 'E' types, that's probably correct.

Here is the bonnet in its component outer parts with most of the repairs done. That's Agip, Henry's boxer, who became a touch jealous after seeing another boxer photographed in our last issue.

Bonnet Repairs

The bonnet on FBV 7D was meant to stay, however. It appeared very sound and fitted with a sense of belonging. Buying a replacement is not simple a matter of painting it and fitting it straight on – there's usually much fettling to be done. For a start, the bonnet always arrives too long which involves trimming the bulkhead end to the right length. At the front end, shims in front and on top of the hinge are fitted and have to be swapped around until the correct line is achieved. A good man will have no trouble in doing this but it could take someone less experienced several days to get it right (or wrong...).

Looking at the overall rust versus the good metal proportions on our 'E' type project, there was no doubting that the favour fell on good metal. We isolated the corroded regions to wing/ centre panel edge returns, a little at the wing bottom corners where they meet the bulkhead and a section on the nose under-tray. The dents will respond to any panel man worth his salt.

It looked as though the under-tray had been driven up a kerb and so we looked at that first. Matt Dewhurst was having a holiday and so Henry drafted in ex-Lynx panel man Mick Clarke in his stead. I didn't expect the tray to come off without a fight but, although it put up token resistance, we soon had it, and the lights and bumpers, removed. Then we saw our first horror. The hidden side of the front off-side bonnet centre section was layered with newspaper (1969 edition) and traces of body filler. My heart sank and I almost admitted defeat and ordered a new bonnet. But Mick decided to look further and find out a little more.

The bonnet under-tray came away without too much of a fight.

Mick was able to gain better access with the under-tray placed on trestles.

Using a flame to heat the metal, the stretching was reduced and the steel shrunk back to normal giving the panel its original 'spring'.

We removed all the internal panels to get greater access. Then with the paper removed the filler could be extracted. We found a number of holes drilled so that a dent puller could be inserted and some minor accident damage repaired. The nature of the repair was amateur in the extreme. Without much thought, the dent had been roughly pulled to shape and then finished with body filler. Using Jenolite paint stripper to remove the top layer, we found it some half an inch thick in places. Criticise it I might, I can't help but be impressed that it lasted all this time but then what would it have looked like had the car been in regular use?

Mick got to work on the lower pan and made a great job of the dents. The metal had stretched somewhat and it was fascinating to watch as he shrunk the panel with his blow torch. The next job was to strip the inside air ducts from the bonnet. With those away we removed each wing and could see whether I had made the right decision to repair and not replace – the centre section/wing flanges are some of the most rust-prone parts on an 'E' type bonnet.

Our first impression had been correct, happily. Most of the wing/centre panel returns were sound apart from the area in the centre; that would need replacing. All the inner panels were piled into my estate car to be stripped at home and I left Mick to it while I moved on to the rear suspension.

Rear end check

I had taken the precaution of checking out the rear suspension for wear before removing it from the car and, with the reassurance from Edward Vanderspar, the previous owner, that much work had indeed been done, I left the main unit in place. The perishables, however, were another thing. I removed all four springs and dampers as well as the brake calipers and then started to wonder what to do with them.

In my deliberations I contacted a couple of old mates, Dick Bradley and Ray Ingman at Classic Spares in Waltham Cross (Tel: 0992 716236). They told me of the huge leaps that Spax had made in recent years and I opted for a full set of their gas-filled adjustable shock absorbers. Just in case the rear springs had gone a bit soggy, I ordered a set of them as well.

The Dunlop caliper pistons have a notoriously short life due to internal corrosion. I thought it would be interesting to see how Classic Spares deal with the situation and went along to the engineering works where the

With the front wings removed from the main bonnet (basic nuts and bolts) the inner air duct assemblies can come away.

Paint stripping is an arduous business anyway but compounded here with half an inch of body filler.

caliper pistons are reconditioned. The answer is, of course, to fit high tensile, continuous cast stainless steel liners.

The idea is that each cylinder is bored out to accept a liner but the trade secret is how the liner is sealed at the base of the cylinder. It is then precisely turned to the correct size to accept the standard piston. Each cylinder spends some time in the blasting cabinet beforehand to achieve a finish suitable for plating. Every unit undergoes a pressure test to a minimum of 2,500psi followed by pulse pressure from 500psi rising in 500psi increments to simulate violent braking. Convinced, I had my set done.

All I need do now is to fit the pistons with new seals and assemble the calipers. I have left the fronts for the time being as I cannot decide if I

This is typical of the rust at the wing edge return. Not enough in my view to consign the bonnet to the scrap heap.

should leave it standard or upgrade to Series 2/420. I can't handle too many decisions in one week.

Back to the metal

By the time I returned to Henry Pearman's, Mick had finished his work on the bonnet. The edge returns had been folded with exactly the same radius as the original. When the wing met the centre section all bolt holes aligned and the top edges ran true. Of course I will not be able to judge how well the bonnet has been done until it is finally fitted to the car.

The majority of the paint had been left on the bonnet for protection, though we had used a magnet to check if there were any other areas of hidden body filler. However, we were satisfied that all the serious repairs had been done. The final finishing will be done in the paint shop.

While I was stripping the inside of the car I detected a trace of water staining from the bulkhead. This was the one thing I didn't want to find. It was clear to me that the water drain tubes inside the main bulkhead had corroded and needed replacement. These days replacements are made of long-lasting copper so, once the job has been done, in theory that's it. But the replacement job is a nightmare even on a bare tub, let alone one with all the wiring and instruments still fitted.

Although Henry had moved to much larger premises some 18 months ago, these are already overflowing. What that means to me is that the paint shop is occupied for some time and time is something I haven't got. So I planned to move the shell straight to another paint shop but, as there is still stripping out to be done, I will bring the car home. At least my garage has been extended at the new house and I took the opportunity to have a Mech-Mate pit installed. A couple of weeks' blitz in my spare time should have it ready to be moved again.

Once machined to oversize, the stainless steel liner can be pressed in to the cylinder.

The old and the new. On the right is how the cylinders come in and on the left is how they go out ready to accept the re-sealed piston.

Spax adjustable gas shock absorbers and new springs are destined for the rear.

Our thanks go to Henry Pearman, Eagle 'E' types (Tel: 0825 830966) for all their help and patience during the work. Shock absorbers and brakes were supplied by Classic Spares Ltd, at Waltham Cross (Tel: 0992 716236).

A new section of metal let in to the bonnet centre panel is almost undetectable and once lead loaded will be as new.

The metal work is finished and we turn to the engine. Jim Patten continues the story

Home at last and ready for the complete strip-down. Front is supported by a small trolley: the Assistant Ed. is not that strong...

PROJECT E-TYPE

t helps to have a realistic target during a rebuild and I've made mine the *Jaguar World* trip to France next May. You'll read about this elsewhere in the issue but to my mind it has to be a must. We're making it an excuse to spend a few days on the Loire after the event. You can make up your own excuse: just be there or you'll regret it later.

I've finally got the 'E' type home ready to strip out before it makes its next trailed journey to the paint shop. I missed the second sill replacement at Henry Pearman's but they kindly took some photographs for me. That side was in remarkable order. Not only were the inner sills perfect but the sill stiffeners were untouched by rust! Exceptional by any standards.

Much as I would have loved to leave the car for them to finish, their schedules would not allow it and, as my 'E' type vacated its slot, so another took its place. So it's thank you time and I am genuinely pleased with the standard of work and treatment I received. It was not just for the press; I

noticed that every one of the many visitors got the same treatment whether buying an 'E' type or talking restorations. Enough of this or I'll be getting soppy next.

I wanted to be able to tell you how we built the engine and how I brought it home ready to be slotted in but there was something along the lines of the best laid plans by mice and men about it. It's not the done thing to knock other people's work when they're not around to defend themselves but the way this engine had been carelessly thrown together was a travesty of motor engineering. Knowing now what an exceptional car it is makes it jar even more.

I'll briefly run you through it, more as a warning of what can happen than anything else. At first glance it appeared that the cylinder head had been skimmed with new valve guides and seats fitted. That was fine, no problem there. The engine block had been re-bored to +.020 and the crankshaft re-ground. The crank had been fitted to the block as had a couple of the pistons. The rest of the parts were still in boxes.

We all have our own favourite engine men; I use Kevin Styles at Series

The inner sill I missed at Henry's. This is after blasting away the surface film of rust – not a trace of corrosion anywhere and just look at those original spot-welds.

crankshaft so it was still presumably full of sludge. When one of the pistons was removed a line was found scored down the big end bearing with a corresponding nick in the crankshaft journal. Obviously what had happened was that, when the piston on its con-rod was lowered into place, it went with a pretty smart jolt and a big end bolt hit the journal. Now the nick is tiny and will polish out but it was so unnecessary. All the other bearings had dust present and none was pre-oiled.

Then Kevin checked the cylinder head out and found the seats and guides to be fine. However, when he fitted the valves that came with the engine he found that the valve clearances were massive, even with the thickest shims fitted. After measuring the valve seats to check their position and much head scratching he examined the valves.

Kevin Styles produced this minor avalanche by prodding around inside the engine block with a screwdriver. This can be the result of a prolonged lay-up period. The previous engine builder was quite happy to leave this in place!

A very slight 'blow' between these cylinders has interrupted the engine build sequence so we have a quiet interlude while the block is re-surfaced.

Original valve on left, pattern valve on right. The difference in height is for real. Always buy genuine Jaguar or approved supplier parts.

That's our crankshaft on the left after Kevin Styles had cleaned out the sludge. On the right is a crankshaft from another engine. See how congealed it is. Never replace a crank without thoroughly cleaning this away.

One Engines. I dropped everything engine related at his workshop and waited his call. When it came, I didn't expect to hear: "You had better get over here and take a look at this lot."

It appears that the engine had been thrown together without a care for detail. To begin with, none of the core plugs had been removed so obviously no attempt had been made to clean the inside of the block. Similarly none of the bungs had been taken out of the

Problem solved. It appears that the valves are slightly shorter than Jaguar's own. Looking carefully, the name 'County' could be seen at the top of the valve stem.

With a set of original Jaguar valves installed, situation normal was achieved. Some may think that my obsession with fitting original supply type parts verges to the point of paranoia but this is precisely the

You may just see a scored line down these big-end bearings. This was caused by a nick on the crank-pin when it was caught by a carelessly-fitted piston.

reason why. The pistons, oil pump and other parts were all in manufacturers' boxes and so we could be reasonably confident of their sourcing.

It was obvious what we would find when the core plugs were popped out. Thick orangey-red muck had compacted at the base of the block. Remember this car had been laid up for 16 years so it was bound to be congealed. The crankshaft was not so bad as the low mileage had not allowed a build-up of sludge although there was some present and should be cleaned. A clogged up cylinder block is one of the major contributing factors to overheating. Clear it during the rebuild and run a quality anti-freeze and it should keep cool for years.

With the crank thoroughly cleaned it was sent over to E.D.S. at South Ockendon for balancing. Apparently one of the connecting rods was quite a

This picture shows the new crankshaft pulley and the flywheel with clutch after balancing. Minor amounts of metal have been removed by either drilling or machining. The pistons were machined from the inside until all weighed-in exactly the same. Note the mark (exaggerated here) on the clutch and flywheel to denote the correct positioning for when the cover plate is finally bolted in place.

With the correct Jaguar valves installed, Kevin had no problems finding valve clearances; indeed they were all very similar as you would expect.

Here's an extremely common problem on the engine front cover. This is the area where the water pump bolts on and a small amount of corrosion has taken place at the bottom where the water lies. It hasn't penetrated yet but I'm taking no chances. I'll pack it off to Alison Atkins at S & A Specialist Welding (Tel: 0702 549658) and have peace of mind.

Extreme care was taken to remove each securing tack so as not to damage the recent hood.

bit heavier than the rest, unusual for Jaguar; they're normally pretty close. I bought a new crankshaft damper (still available from Jaguar for the 4.2) as this is particularly important. Perished rubber bonding can prove disastrous, setting up peculiar harmonics that can actually fracture a crankshaft.

Everything from the damper through pistons and rods to flywheel and clutch pressure plate was balanced. That's as far as we have got. Kevin noticed a very slight blow-by between two bores so the block will have a slight skim to make the surface perfect. Certainly by the next issue we shall have the engine built.

Back home with the carburettors on the bench, I decided to overhaul these myself. Again they are in pretty good order with very little wear on the throttle spindles. The worst problem is that moisture has got into all the little corners, making what little movement there is a bit creaky. The choke slides, for instance, are solid. Unlike most

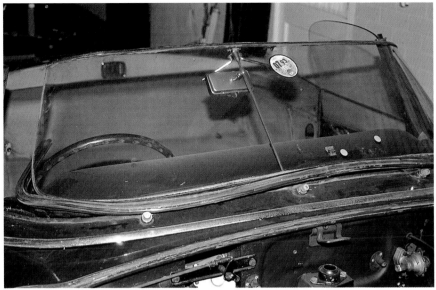

The windscreen came out quite readily once the top rail was removed. With the dash top removed I could see into the bulkhead and came to the realisation that the dash itself would also have to come out to replace the inner water rails.

Call me obsessive if you will but there's nothing like genuine parts when replacement is necessary.

other Jaguars, the 'E' type has a manual choke. When the lever is pulled, a brass rod moves down through the carburettor body to lower the jet and enrich the mixture. These three were going nowhere.

Although not perished, the diaphragm around the jet was looking a little fragile. Seems like Burlen Fuel Services will be hearing the sound of my credit card number again... I've put the carburettors back in their box until I've stripped the shell out; at least I now know what I need.

Over to the bodyshell. First to come off is the hood and windscreen. They are both vulnerable (the hood is new) and in the way. Usually during a rebuild the hood is just pulled of but this one is to be refitted. Wood is used inside the rear bulkhead for the hood to be tacked on to. Each tiny little tack was levered out in turn without doing any damage to the hood. It worked. Two bolts each side secure the hood frame. I marked these and placed them in a safe place that I will

actually find again as these bolts are shouldered and unique to this application.

The windscreen came out quite readily. Chrome catches at each end and the mirror stem in the centre hold the top rail down. With these released the rail lifts off and the screen can be eased out. I put mine in the attic. It's warm and dry up there. The top rail is pretty twisted because I think the screen had been changed and the rail levered off in the process. I will need a new rail but it must be a perfect fit. If the fit is poor, it is likely to crack the screen.

I now had access to the padded dash top. Four nuts hold these brackets to the bulkhead. The top is unmarked so it was simply cleaned and put up in the attic with the other parts.

The way was now clear to seek out those heater pipes hidden in the depths of the bulkhead. It rather looks as though the dash may have to come out to get access. I might have to ask

See how each hood bolt is shouldered to act as a pivot pin on the hood frame.

Mike Harris of LWR to pop in on the pretext of opening a bottle of Nuits Saint George. Pulling that lot out with one hand while holding a camera in the other looks a mite acrobatic to me.

The rear bumpers are proving a bit of a problem because the plates holding the bolts have chosen to spin. I'll have to put a little bit of heat on the nuts when I get my gas bottles out of storage

It pays to keep an eye on the classifieds. I found a pair of original rear light units still in their Lucas boxes, advertised in the Jaguar Enthusiast club magazine. Must keep looking for the fronts now.

In the next issue we will have the engine built and the body finally stripped. The front suspension has been rebuilt but, after the engine saga, I've decided to strip it down and do it again. There have been too many spurious parts leaking on to the market and I will feel happy only when original Jaguar stock is fitted.

Thanks as ever to: Henry Pearman's Eagle 'E' Types (Tel: 0825 830966); Series One Engines (Tel: 081-597 3079); E.D.S. (Tel: 0708 857108).

It's not just 'E' types that are cared for at Henry Pearman's, these wagtails should have a peaceful upbringing.

PROJECT E-TYPE

Engine, front suspension and paint. Jim Patten reports on his 4.2 roadster restoration.

Kevin Styles of Series One Engines had a bad feeling about the 'E' type engine. Something didn't feel right with the block. Although it had supposedly been bored to +0.20in, Kevin's mistrust got the better of him and he measured every bore almost without thinking. Whatever instinct he had proved right. Each one measured differently!

"You're all right, though," he said with a wry grin, "they're all slightly small which means I can still bore them to the right size." In fact, as an experiment, we put all the pistons in the bores up to the rings. There was one bore where the piston would barely fit. Imagine the problems of trying it with the piston rings compressed. If all of the pistons had gone in then the engine would hardly have made it down the road.

With all the reciprocating parts back from balancing at EDS, Kevin began to build the engine proper. There were no dramas, everything went back as it should except that is, when it came to checking the timing marks. I had bought a new crankshaft

There's always a stubborn one. This winder mechanism retaining screw would not budge whatever was thrown at it and so its head was cut off. The remains will be drilled out later.

damper from Jaguar and, although it was identical to the original 'E' type in specification, the timing marks are in a different place. Whereas the 'E' type timing pointer is on the lower sump, on later Jaguars it is located on a bracket fixed to the front timing chain cover.

Knowing at this stage meant that Kevin could fit a later bracket. After establishing TDC (top dead centre), the bracket was mounted exactly by the timing marks and centre punched in place. We've had a couple of calls at the office about this damper because some Jaguar parts departments have said they cannot supply for the 'E' type. Ask them for the XJ 4.2 application and, subject to the timing pointer being changed, the damper is the same.

We had a slight puzzle over the cylinder head chrome 'D' washers – there weren't any. We could find no evidence or tell-tale marks on the cylinder head that any had been fitted. The only clues we could find were slight indentations where round washers had been. I am pretty confident that the engine had never been apart before so, although I have boxes of spare 'D' washers, I chose not to replace them and instead go with how it seemed to have come from Browns Lane.

Kevin gave the cam covers a light buff (avoiding that inappropriate chrome-like finish) while I bought new chrome head and cam cover nuts from Classic Spares. With detail painting to the block and a good finish to the sump and other alloy parts, the finished unit looks very pleasing. I only hope I am able to keep it somewhere near this condition when it's fitted. Just

a thought – if you are rebuilding your car, try to leave the engine until you really need it otherwise that nicely rebuilt unit will be sitting around the workshop for possibly a couple of years (18 in the case of my Mk V – Ed.) allowing all sorts of internal nasties to develop. Leaving oil seals dry is one of the worst things you can do – leaks

will be almost inevitable.

With the obvious problems found on the engine, I now wanted to look at the suspension, rebuilt by the same unknown hand. It had been painted black and, as the original finish should be a silver cadmium plate, I felt the effort in dismantling to be justified.

Sure enough, the demon had struck again. This car had not been driven anywhere and yet the ball joint rubber boots had cracked. Had there been any grease inside it most certainly would have eased out. But it hadn't – yes, that's right, there was a positive absence of grease in the ball joints which had been assembled dry! I've no idea where the ball joints or suspension bushes came from and so I had no alternative but to renew them all.

The suspension upright came off in the familiar way, top nut undone first, followed by simultaneous hammer blows each side of the upright to release the ball joint. Three or four blows had the job done. This was repeated for the bottom and the upright came away. The top wishbone is held to the side frame by two threaded blocks bolted to the frame. The wishbone in turn is bolted to the

Despite an attempt at sabotage, the 'E' type engine is finally rebuilt. Kevin Styles gives the cylinder head nuts a final tighten.

Although 'E' type dampers are no longer available, a 4.2 XJ6 type can be used but the timing marks appear in a different place. This can be overcome by using the XJ6 timing pointer on the timing chain cover.

The top wishbone is held to the front frame by three bolts to this mounting block. Shims in between control the camber.

blocks. A similar system exists at the bottom. Camber shims are fitted between the mounting bracket and the block. I retained the shims with their respective mounting blocks and would use them as a starting point when the suspension is set up later. The torsion bars had already been removed.

I haven't the time to continue with the suspension at the moment as the body needs to be stripped for painting. My bottle of Chateau d'Lure worked and I finally tempted Mike Harris of LWR to remove the old heater and vacuum pipes from inside the bulkhead. He managed it while leaving the dash assembly intact. There

There are cracks in that new ball joint rubber boot and it's supposed to be new! When the joint was opened up there was no grease inside either.

are not many people I would trust these days but I do wish I could afford to give the entire project over to Mike and sit at home studying the attributes of Pinot Noir.

Stripping a car down is almost a case of following your nose; the doors gave readily of their internals although one screw proved to be immovable and I resorted to cutting off its head. I'll drill out the stub later.

Moving to the boot area, I had no real need to evict the fuel tank and knew I would be in for a fight but went for it anyway. The boot catch and tank mounting bracket should be removed first. The bracket bolts are located at the other side of the boot floor in the gap between it and the axle. I didn't even try to wriggle the fuel filler pipe off the tank but cut it with a Stanley knife down its length. It would be replaced as a matter of course and so there was no point in fighting.

I had a real problem with the sump (that little tube at the bottom of the tank housing a filter with a drain plug at the bottom); no matter what I did, it would not shift. Eventually I resorted to a chain wrench but all that did was to distort the tube. In the end I used a hammer and chisel and, although it cut into the wall, the sump did give and I was able to unthread the now scrap remains.

Now came the almost impossible job of getting the tank out of the car. I struggled for ages and then, without so much as a murmur, it gave up and slipped over the boot floor. When the

There's absolutely no point in trying to remove the fuel filler hose. Just cut it down its length and it will slip off without trouble. After all, it's going to be replaced anyway.

Not even a chain wrench would move the fuel tank sump. Only a chisel got it started but by then the tube was only so much scrap and needed replacement.

floor beneath the tank has been treated I think I will replace the tank then and fully mask it rather than risk damaging the rest of the newly painted floor area.

Now that my gas bottles are back I was able at last to get at the rear bumpers. With some serious heat on the nuts, they gave without resistance and I finally had all the chrome off. I was getting close to dispatching the car to the paint shop; choosing a good one was difficult but when Mike Harris at LWR puts a recommendation forward I listen, so the mere fact that he thought Bert Tyler at Apollo Autos was worth more than a second look was enough for me.

Bert came to my home to give the 'E' type a look over and it was fascinating to see his reaction when he looked at the usual rot areas only to find good metal and original welds. Thankfully there were not the usual derogatory remarks about other people's work; instead he was actually

Bert Tyler at Apollo Autos starts to paint-strip a door. Note that he puts a thin piece of masking tape around the edge and beneath the door handle hole to prevent stripper from getting into the inside of the door. What paint is left underneath this will be sanded off using a light grade of paper later.

Ten minutes later the door is down to metal. See how well Matt Dewhurst repaired the lower part of the skin. Despite a continuous MIG weld there is no distortion at all and Bert had no trouble preparing it for paint.

very complimentary about Matt Dewhurst's work, which I found refreshing.

Because I was still to remove the front frames for a little more rust protection around the mounts, I began by taking just the doors and bootlid to Apollo. I had anticipated stripping the paint myself but, as Bert wanted to minimise the amount of time the shell spent without paint, he would do the stripping. He was a little sceptical about the Jenolite paint stripper I provided but soon changed his view once he started using it. The first door was down to the metal in ten minutes flat. Mind you, it had seen only factory paint, never having been resprayed.

Micro-blisters are the paint shops' most fearsome enemy. A finished car can look good only to sprout pimples six months later. One of the causes is water settling on bare metal or being absorbed into primer. Even modern primers, supposedly resistant to

moisture, are seemingly not immune. Bert's answer is to work on each section separately under controlled conditions and, as soon as the repairs are done and primer laid on, spray a protective top colour coat. Then, when the whole car has been treated (with trial fits along the way), the final

preparation, paint and finishing is done. Sounds good practice to me.

We commandeered the conservatory at home for a weekend and Karen had a go at the seats using Connolly cleaner and hide food. There are no splits or tears and the piping is intact without any of the usual wear signs down the driver's edge. Perhaps the only indication of age is on the back of the seat but it is only minimal. Edward Vanderspar's wife (the car's previous owner) had made a good job Connollising the seats as the grey has retained its colour well.

The bumpers will be needed soon to check conformity of line around the bonnet, so they are being dispatched to the chromer while the suspension parts go in a different direction to be plated. In the next issue the bodyshell will be in the paint shop where we will finally strip all the paint and see what is really underneath.

My thanks go to Dick Bradley and Ray Ingman at Classic Spares Ltd (Tel: 01992 716236), Mike Harris at LWR (Tel: 01708 375425) and to Bert Tyler of Apollo Autos, Coppen Road, off Selinas Lane, Dagenham, Essex RM8 1HJ (Tel: 0181-517 0926).

In the Patten conservatory, Karen gets to work on the seats. The results are extremely pleasing with a soft and supple finish to the leather.

PROJECT E-TYPE

Jim Patten's 4.2 Roadster returns from the paint shop

Home at last: the 'E' type arrives on the back of John Harris's transporter.

It's an unreal environment inside the blasting chamber. The protective suit adds to the lunar feel as the front underpan is blasted.

Spot the difference. What looks like grey primer on the left is in fact the bare metal after blasting at Anglia Rustguard. It is impossible to clean metal like this by hand.

There's nothing like curling up in front of a fire with a drink and a good book. Well I haven't an open fire, so the central heating will have to serve. But my reading is the 4.2 'E' type parts book and my drink an excellent '84 Chateau Moulin Saint-Georges.

I had decided to make a complete list of every part that I needed and pass the lot over to Classic Spares to deal with. You may make some small saving by shopping around for every last bit but it will save a lot of time if you let one of the several good parts suppliers compile your wants. Then I would still end up using nearby Classic for quite a lot anyway and I knew that they don't make you pay through the nose.

I took the bonnet underpan section and the inner air ducts along to Anglia Rustguard in Braintree for sand blasting. They handle all sorts of materials and are quite used to old cars. They were already working on a pre-war saloon and a full Fiat 124 Spyder bodyshell. If there are any weak points in the metal then you have to accept that holes will appear.

When I walked in to the blasting room, it was rather like walking on a lunar beach with all that fine sand underfoot and and lighting akin to moon-glow. Using the right type of sand along with the correct regulated pressure (unskilled use of the process can easily ripple a panel beyond redemption), every speck of rust and

paint was removed. One or two minor blemishes were found but I was pleased that they could be repaired at this stage.

They then applied a tough, industrial primer seemingly unavailable for us DIYers. I was extremely pleased with the results and the fact that no distortion had taken place. Anglia are currently investigating a low pressure technique using plastics that is capable of stripping paint layer by layer or isolated areas as thin as a pencil line. The trade has come a long way.

Back in my workshop I set to and reassembled the bonnet ready for transportation. When new, the under-bonnet air ducts are bonded to the bonnet centre section as well as bolted front and rear. Knowing that there were numbers of extremely competent modern sealers on the market, I decided to meet up with my local 3M guy to find out what was available, not just for this job but other applications

Bert Tyler made small work of the dent in the rear wing. So great was the number of smaller dents that the work soon grew monotonous. Fortunately the car had never been resprayed and only the original paint needed stripping, not such a laborious task.

The individual wishbone components had been assembled and here, the top ball pin goes into the greased wishbone. The ball seat had previously been examined for wear and passed.

as well.

There is a structural adhesive available that is probably too effective for the job. It can actually be used to fit wheelarch repair panels so thorough is its bond. Finally (after consultation) I opted for their Metal to Metal adhesive, specifically designed for bonding bonnet stiffeners and anti-flutter applications but not high stress bonding.

One item that was to prove an absolute saviour was their Clean 'n Strip discs. The material clears all paint and surface rust but leaves the metal alone. It's very flexible and can get into some really awkward spots. Scotch-Brite pads are great for cleaning all sorts of parts, particularly rust oxidisation from clean metal.

I also liked the look of their wax rust-proofer in an aerosol can with a micro-bore extension nozzle. I used this to get into the front engine frames. If you look at the inner faces of the frames where they bolt to the bulkhead you will see a very small hole. The aerosol was perfect for this. I know that many people have trouble getting hold of 3M products because they are sold only through trade outlets. But most of these factors will sell direct to the public so give the likes of Brown Brothers (use your Yellow Pages) a visit.

Many people have different ideas of how the engine frames should be treated. The favourite is to paint them off the car and fit with new plated bolts with washers. I stuck with the most recognised factory method. As the 'E' type went down the production line it was assembled to a state prior to painting. The frames were then fitted but certain bolts left off to hold cable or pipe clips. No washers were fitted. It's quite easy to do – just make a note as the car is taken apart or take photographs. I also used Dum Dum (a sort of sealer that doesn't stick, just

With the top seat in place (minus the spring), shims and the top plate are followed with shims added or subtracted until the ball moves freely.

seals) between the frame and bulkhead, as Jaguar did. Many do not like to see the excess squidging out from the frames but that, folks, is how they came. Anyway, most of the excess can be carefully cut away afterwards.

I tried ordering new bonnet bolts from Jaguar but of course they were NLA. Just opposite Appollo's are a company called Carona Engineering Supply, nut and bolt suppliers, and, after a lot of searching, I found the ones I wanted. I later learnt that Classic Spares sell the whole lot, nuts, bolts, spacers and washers, sorted in a bag...

I was not surprised to find that the bonnet did not fit as perfectly as it did when it first came off. You can't strip a lump as big as the bonnet and expect everything to remain constant. It would have to wait until the car arrived at Appollo.

John Harris at Alpha Autos is no stranger to 'E' types. He has owned and restored them for years so he was a safe choice when it came to transporting the car. Despite the shell's lack of back wheels, he was sufficiently skilled and equipped to make the job look easy.

With the car on its way I had the suspension to build. The parts had just returned from the zinc platers. I decided to put the chrome plating on hold until it had all been offered up to the refinished car, just to make sure. It was a delight to be working with the clean parts; they felt like new. I was right to have been suspicious of the parts previously used as the ball joint lower seat was made of a most peculiar material. I discarded the whole lot and replaced with new.

The top ball joint lower seat is part of the upper wishbone and, if this wears, then the wishbone needs replacing. They are available in reconditioned form however. Mine were good (what did you expect!) and so just needed assembling. A thin layer of grease was applied followed by the ball pin and then its top seat. Shims

I concocted a novel way of fitting the top circlip. Using a socket fitted on the grease nipple, I used a valve spring compressor (the deep recess type) to push against the spring, making the circlip fit a doddle. The rubber boot followed.

I was not happy with the lower ball seat material and so used a new bottom ball joint kit of the fibrous type.

determine the end float and they are held by a large end plate that carries a grease nipple. The assembly is secured by a circlip. There is an end-float figure but really what we are looking for is the ability for the ball to move in the seats without resistance but no slop. Adding or subtracting shims satisfies this.

Once that has been achieved, the shims and plate are removed, a liberal amount of grease applied everywhere and a spring inserted in the top ball pin seat. Then there's the fun of compressing the spring while trying to fit the circlip. I had a brain-wave and used a valve spring compressor. It's quite easy really. A thin, deep socket the size of the grease nipple is located on the nipple. Then (it has to be a compressor for recessed valves) the valve spring end of the compressor is

A new upper ball seat is pressed in to the lower ball joint area of the suspension upright.

The ball pin is greased and fitted to the seat. A nominal amount of shims is used and the lower cap fitted. Shims are added or subtracted until the ball pin moves freely without any slack.

placed over the ball pin with the screw end over the deep socket. Compress the ball joint spring and insert the circlip at your leisure. That's today's handy hint. The outer rubber boot then slides over the pin and is held by a clip. I still prefer the early black boots (no, it's not a fetish – you really don't want to know what mine is!) to the later clear with their silly plastic retainers.

The bottom ball joints are easiest dealt with by using sealed XJ40 type though I continued in the old tradition and fitted the original type. The 'new' ball seat had been prised out and discarded along with the ball pin and top seat. The new top seat taps in to the steering upright. I used a socket of the same diameter to drift it home. The fibrous bottom seat is also tapped in place but with a little more care as the material isn't designed to be hit. Another thin smear of grease was put on the ball pin and it was placed in the top seat.

Using a nominal number of shims, the bottom cup is offered up and adjusted by use of shims until a similar state of movement as was gained on the top is achieved. Lock plates are fitted beneath the bolts and the black boots slid over the pin.

By this time, Bert Tyler had been getting on with the bodyshell. His comments about the number of dents

Back at the paint shop, the 'E' type has just had its primer applied in the oven.

could not possibly be printed here but all I saw was straight metal where there had previously been a mess. Using a variety of dollies and hammers he tapped away until he was completely satisfied. I think even he was surprised at the amount of time it took.

The rear underpan was a difficult section. It must seem almost unreasonable to make this area perfect because few people actually see it but it's a credit to Bert that he took the amount of trouble that he did. The bonnet was another thing. We had to re-shim the front to get the perfect alignment. Luckily, all the bolts gave without shearing and we were able to establish the position we wanted. Those readers tiring of hearing how good this car is can take some comfort in the fact that when Bert finally stripped the paint off, he found a small section of rust on one lower rear quarter panel. It was an easy repair and presented no problems.

It was then a matter of carrying out all the refinishing and offering up the chrome to be sure of a perfect fit. It is not unusual to have to grind a little from the bumper bars and you don't want to be doing that with newly-chromed parts.

Sticking to the original plan, the shell was wheeled into the oven and warmed before applying ICI long life etching primer followed by ICI acrylic primer. Off with the bonnet again to treat the frames and bulkhead along with the inside of the bonnet. Bert had used the 3M metal adhesive earlier to get the air ducts finally fixed. All the bonnet catches had been removed for zinc plating except the bracket on the bulkhead; that remains in body colour.

The boot area was the first to be put in colour. I wanted to fit the tank now and save the possibility of damaging the paint later. With the area thoroughly Waxoyled and the tank bottom treated too, I was ready for the trial. Just as I was jockeying for position, the tank slid into place without a murmur. What was I

With the 'E' type in colour, the front suspension is bolted to the frames (without the torsion bars) ready to receive the front wheels when the splined hubs are fitted

worrying about? Bert comprehensively masked the tank and I put that on my 'forget for now' list.

The next time I saw the car it was all blue with Bert flatting the body. He had used a modern two-pack paint from ICI. This, and all the primers had been supplied through the local, Selinas Lane, Dagenham branch of Brown Brothers. Remember that Jaguar used a synthetic paint (not cellulose) from the early 1950s so a modern two-pack is not so different from the original as you may think. Certainly the colour was spot on. It was finished by the time I called next and yes, I was thrilled. It will sit there a little longer while I bolt the suspension on so that it can return home on all four wheels.

In the meantime I had better get my act together. It's the end of March as I write this and the French trip is approaching fast. I can only pray that the little elves from the nursery rhymes come out at night and help me along, just as they did the cobbler.

Acknowledgements:
Alpha Autos (Tel: 0836 232114)
Anglia Rustguard (Tel: 01376 344683)
Appollo Autos, Coppen Road, off Selinas Lane, Dagenham, Essex RM8 1HJ (Tel: 0181 517 0926)
Brown Brothers, Coppen Road, Selinas Lane, Dagenham, Essex RM8 1QH (Tel: 0181 593 8811)
Classic Spares Ltd., (Tel: 01992 716236)
3M products available through trade motor factors.

PROJECT E-TYPE

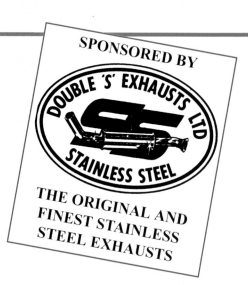

SPONSORED BY

DOUBLE 'S' EXHAUSTS LTD
STAINLESS STEEL

THE ORIGINAL AND
FINEST STAINLESS
STEEL EXHAUSTS

*Jim Patten has a severe case of the hiccups as the
reassembly continues against the clock*

F rom out of chaos and confusion, peace and order are bound to prevail, I tell myself. Or are they? The atmosphere in the Patten household has been decidedly heavy over the past few weeks. By the time this issue hits the bookstalls we will all know whether the project 'E' type has been completed in time for the *Jaguar World* trip to France or whether the XK had to be dusted down.

I had a nagging doubt in the back of my mind over the door hinges. The passenger side was fine but the driver's had just a little slop in it. I reasoned that as wear had started it could only accelerate. Uneasy with them, I took the hinges to Avon Engineering where Tim Smith drilled them through and fitted new bronze bushes. The original was just a steel pin running through the aluminium hinge. I managed to get them to Appollo just in time for the doors to be fitted.

Back home in the comfort of my own garage, I thought that I would have a clear run ahead. Daunting, yes, but at least I was in control. Before the

I think that I need to move into the garage and sleep in the corner if the 'E' type is to be ready for the Entente Cordial trip to France

It may only appear slightly different but the problems caused by the 'repro' pipe's incorrect radius and the protrusion into the bulkhead caused considerable problems.

The tie rod has been adjusted in the ball housing. The resistance on the rod should equate to 7lb on a spring balance scale.

A slot provides access for a drift to punch out the old bearing seat in the front hub.

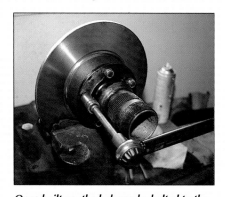

Once built up, the hub can be bolted to the new disc. Don't be alarmed, I've used old brake pads each side of the disc so that the jaws of the vice will do no damage.

A new circlip secures the replacement universal joint on the steering column shaft. The method for replacing these is exactly the same as you would a prop shaft.

This pimple on the new steering column bush locates it in the housing. Although it is a push fit, it will need a little help to get the location right.

Watch out for splits in the steering column housing around the welds on the yolk. These were fine.

engine went in, all the parts around the bulkhead needed to be fitted, including those dreaded heater pipes. The original pipes had split but they would have been replaced as a matter of course anyway. As for the vacuum pipes, they were in virtually new condition and would 'go again'. Trying to persuade the bottom pipe to travel down into the depths of the bulkhead was a real struggle but somehow when I finally did get it in situ, it just didn't seem to fit right.

I decided on a trial fit of all pipes but was soon halted when I discovered that the vacuum pipe that piggy-backs the heater pipe would never fit correctly as the water pipe was too proud. So it all had to come out again. Silly me, I should have compared the new pipe to the old before even thinking of fitting it. Not only was there too much pipe protruding inside the bulkhead but the radius to the flange manifold was wrong as well – instead of a tight radius there was more of a

sweeping bend passing through the flange at an angle. The only way to rectify this was to put a bar of exactly the same diameter inside the pipe and gently move it until it was at right angle with the flange.

The upper pipes were not so bad and eventually they all went in correctly. I had received the zinc plating back from Mike Harris at LWR and was able to reassemble the heater control valve. The internals are available now but mine looked OK so I just put it all back together with the merest suggestion of silicone sealer around the diaphragm. A new seal was fitted, again with a touch of silicone sealer around the water pipe, just in case. I wondered as I fitted the screen washer jets what would happen if these needed replacing at some later stage for they are all but impossible to reach with the screen and dash-top fitted.

Rightly or wrongly, I decided to go with the original wiring loom but I'm having trouble with the decision. It's on

the cards that a new loom will be fitted at the end of the season as wiring can get brittle with age and I don't think I'll ever be happy until it's done. Of course it's almost impossible to see the original colours on the braided wires, so I took the precaution of identifying certain problem areas. When the windscreen wiper motor went back, for instance, each wire was marked to the corresponding one in the loom.

The motor itself is held in the bulkhead by four bolts. When I was at Corona Engineering I bought a quantity of plated nuts and bolts so that all the replacements were new. On the 'E' type, the wiper control is by rod and link rather than the more familiar worm cable. It's quite easy to fit as it just pops on to the wiper linkage. I didn't think it worth removing all the linkage as it all felt in good condition so I had just let it rest beneath the bulkhead top panel. Classic Spares supplied new wiper spindle chromes and nuts.

Now was the time to replace the broken heater control cable. It comes extra long and has to be trimmed to size. I opted to use the original outer cable because it is partly covered with plastic and is, of course, the right length. The inner was easily cut to size. New grommets were fitted too. A good number of these are still available from Jaguar but perhaps the easiest way to buy them is in a complete car kit. The little glove box could go in now as the top nuts that hold this are virtually inaccessible with the dash top on.

Forward now to the unfinished steering. Edward Vanderspar, the previous owner, had put new bushes in the steering rack. I carried on where he had left off, checking the outer tie rods. The ball pin was fine and so it was just greased and put back in the socket. This is adjustable by a lock nut on the ball housing. To get the exact amount of resistance in the tie rod, a spring balance should be attached to the end of the tie rod. The rod should lift at 7lb. Rack gaiters are still available from Jaguar so I fitted these followed by new track rod ends.

New rack mounts had come with the car and the Metalastik name was clearly seen so I was happy to use them. They bolt to the front frame first. On the outer metal section there is a large hole. A long bolt passes through this. Looking at it side on from the head, there should be a washer, locknut and finally the fixing nut. The idea is that the lock nut holds the inner metal section to the frame. The bolt head and washer should just have clearance between the metal section.

I couldn't bear the thought of bleeding the brakes inboard and so I have fitted these bleed nipple extensions.

The newly-painted radius arm with new bushes fitted. It does actually mean removing the lower fulcrum shaft to get to the locating bolt but that's as far as I went.

See how the carbon on the old release bearing (left) has vanished completely. The replacement is a Borg & Beck.

Should the rubber mount shear at any time, then the bolt acts as a safety link so that the rack is not thrown completely off. It happened to me once. Although alarming, it does give you a chance to stop the car under control.

The steering column shaft is in two parts. One long stretch with a universal joint at the end, the other just a couple joint to steering wheel end. I fitted new U/Js as a matter of course. It was interesting that the manufacturer's part number is the same as that for the MGB. New steering column bushes were fitted into the casing. The old ones were just pushed out and the new pushed in. There are a couple of rubber pimples that locate in holes in the casing to secure them. I'll fit the steering column assembly once the engine is in.

Both front and rear splined hubs were in remarkable condition so I stripped the front of their old bearings and replaced with new. There is a slot inside the hub to get a drift in and

hammer the old bearings out. Ideally the new bearings should be pressed in but few of us have these facilities and so we resort to the bench, brass drifts and hammers. With a new oil seal and plenty of grease, the hub is put back on the stub axle. The nut should be turned until it kisses home and then backed off until the hub spins freely. A new split pin should always be used.

Moving backwards (how fast this seems when you're writing it), the rear end had to come down again to treat the underside with Waxoyl underbody compound. While it was down, I fitted extensions to take the brake bleed nipples to the outside of the frame to make life easier later. I had a new handbrake cable to fit as well but, after an age of fiddling, decided not to. The trouble was that the outer cable was larger than the original. That's OK except it will not fit in the pinch fork in the handbrake. I tried fettling away at the cable and by stretching the fork it went in.

Next problem was the handbrake warning light bracket. That would not fit over the opened fork. My only recourse was to drill out an enlarged hole on the fork and I was not prepared to do that. When I checked the length of both inner cables; they were more or less identical so I gave it up as a bad job and put the original back.

I now had the chance to fit new radius arm bushes as, although Edward had done quite a lot of work to the rear end, these had not needed changing at that time. Well, they do now. I hate

doing this job. The bushes never push out cleanly and eventually a hack-saw blade has to come into play to cut down the length of the metal part of the bush. Great care is needed so as not to cut into the radius arm itself. I usually get it pretty close and then follow up with a sharp chisel.

I've never had the luxury of a pit before and it certainly makes putting the rear end back a lot easier. Using an air ratchet and standing in the pit, the bolts are wizzed up in seconds.

Looking at the prop shaft, I don't think the bearings had ever been changed. I gave it a good clean down and a coating of Jenolite just to remove the top rust and then fitted new universal joints. I expected to see a pile of rusty needles but they actually looked quite fresh.

Edward Vanderspar assured me that the gearbox was in fine fettle and, looking at the condition of the gears, he's absolutely right. So I simply changed the oil, fitted a new top gasket and put the cover back. The clutch was pretty shot though. There was no carbon in the bearing at all. After replacing the three-part clutch (the diaphragm had already been balanced with the rest of the engine) the gearbox was bolted to the engine. The clutch hydraulic slave cylinder and pipework should be fitted now as it's a nightmare to do on the car.

There's a whole heap of things to tell you about yet but I've run out of pages. I guess the car will be finished well before its story is told. At least I hope so!

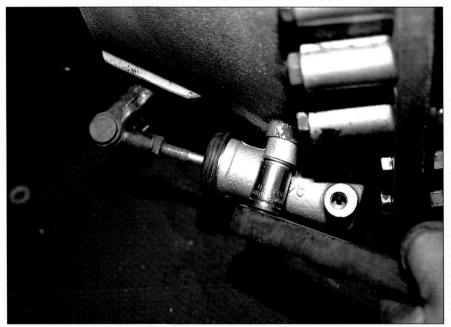

Always fit the clutch slave cylinder and pipes before the engine and gearbox are fitted to the car.

PROJECT E-TYPE
Engine in!

Jim Patten is almost there as the clock ticks away

The trouble with these types of restoration stories is that they inevitably become a series of historical events, with suspense difficult to maintain because of the retrospective manner in which they are told. So, although there is a good deal more to tell, I am delighted to relate that our 'E' type was finished in time for the *Jaguar World* Entente Cordial trip to France – by the skin of our grinding teeth (there will be a separate story of our trip in the next issue). But now, let us rewind the clock and return to our partially-built 'E' type.

Something that Paul Skilleter and I have in common is (among other things) having Paul Roach as a friend which I am sure in time PR will regret. Knowing that PR had been helping our esteemed Ed. with his SS saloon, I promptly nabbed him to help out with the 'E' type too; after all, what are friends for? PR is currently creating a replica of the Mike Hawthorn 3.4 Mk 1 saloon and I must admit to a slight wobble at the knees every time I see it.

With my old buddy to help out I seemed to get a new burst of energy. I had looked at the exhaust manifolds wondering what to do with them. Sure I liked the original enamel but only when new. As far as I know, nobody has achieved an enamel finish that lasts. Double 'S' produce a wonderful six-branch but they needed to fit it to the car and that was impossible just now.

Up from the bottom is JP's favoured way of fitting an 'E' type engine.

Anglia Rustguard came to my rescue. They have a process of spraying molten aluminium directly on to the metal. It is capable of withstanding extremely high temperatures. The only down side is the colour, natural aluminium. Pigments can be added but then the high temperature resistance lowers. What the hell, I went for it anyway; I could always change later, I thought.

Before I sent the manifolds for blasting, I removed the old studs. Each corner is heated to cherry red using an oxy-acetylene torch and then the studs can be wound out using Mole grips. No drilling required and the new studs

This bracket supports the carburettor spindle shaft. A washer of a smaller internal diameter than the original has been welded in the centre to take a throttle bush from an XJS, a much sturdier item.

The weight balance is about right here as the engine is lifted into position ready for the engine mounts to be fitted.

Gorgeous polished stainless steel Double 'S' exhaust set against the dark blue bodywork. I hope that I am up to the job of keeping them that way.

It is essential that the stabiliser mount is correctly adjusted under the full engine weight to avoid vibration coming through the car and damage to the bulkhead bracket.

can be screwed into the original threads.

I've always put 'E' type (and Mk 2 and 'S' type etc. come to that) engines in from underneath and will continue to do so. I have made a trolley to make the negotiation of the engine that much easier. So Paul and I raised the 'E' type at the front until we had sufficient clearance to slide the engine beneath

the frames. The engine was bereft of its mounts and oil filter but with the starter motor fitted. When the engine was roughly in place we gently lowered the car, moving the trolley on its multi-direction castors as we sought for the optimum position. The car rested on axle stands and we then brought the engine crane in to lift the engine up to the engine mounts.

By doing it this way, any possibility of scratching paint on the frames from lowering the engine from above is avoided. It sometimes takes a couple of tries to get the right point of balance though. I've found it to be somewhere before the last engine lifting bracket on the cylinder head. Achieve this and the engine/gearbox should lift up true.

Be careful to ensure that the stabiliser rod (mounted on top of the gearbox bell-housing) passes through the bracket on the bulkhead. With one of us steadying the crane, the other fitted the front engine mounts. There was a little pushing and tugging but they went on without too much trouble. The secret is to keep the engine slightly lifted. Once the weight of the engine is on a mount then it will not move no matter how much you push or lever.

At the gearbox end is a small crossmember. A pin in the gearbox end housing passes though a large spring sandwiched between the gearbox and crossmember. This is compressed and a large washer and split-pin holds it down. A jack will be needed to close the spring further so that the crossmember can be bolted to the car's underside. At this stage, the engine stabiliser (on the bulkhead) will not be touched. The full weight of the engine is needed before this can be fitted. Many make the mistake of thinking that it is a further mount and wind the bottom threaded washer right up. All this does is to rip the bracket off the bulkhead.

The carburettors had been stripped

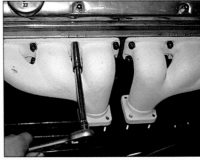

What do you think? A little on the bright side perhaps. At least now they're fitted they are beginning to tone down a bit. At least the finish will not crack off though.

New needles, jets/diaphragm and spring and gaskets were all that was needed on the carburettors.

and deemed OK. No wear in the carbs, spindles or bushes and so they were just reassembled with new needles and jet/diaphragms (supplied by Burlen Fuel Systems) along with the lower spring. Dashpots and inlet manifold had been polished. The distributor too was in fine fettle and, apart from replacing the points, condenser and rotor arm, it was fitted to the engine with a new distributor cap and leads and set at a static timing of nine degrees BTDC.

The heater hoses were fitted beneath the manifold before the carburettors were bolted to the head. A reconditioned water pump was bought through the good offices of Classic Spares.

With the full weight now on the engine (including oil) the engine stabiliser was adjusted. A new rubber stabiliser mount was fitted on the bulkhead bracket. Using a long, thin screwdriver, the threaded lower washer was wound up the thread of the stabiliser rod until it just kissed the bottom of the mount. Then the top seating washer, Nyloc nut and washer were fitted and fully tightened. Job done without any loading on the top mount or bulkhead.

With the engine in place, I could begin to mount the ancillaries around it and on the bulkhead, which, among other things, is what I'll be recounting in the next issue.

Acknowledgments in this issue go to: Anglia Rustguard Ltd (Tel: 01376 344683); Double 'S' Exhaust Ltd (Tel: 01884 33454); Burlen Fuel Systems (Tel: 01722 412500); Classic Spares Ltd, Unit 4 Brook Road, Brittania Road, Waltham Cross, Herts. EN8 7NP (Tel: 01992 716236).

PROJECT E-TYPE
The engine runs!

Although Jim Patten had his heart in his mouth when it didn't fire first time.

I feel a little cheated now that the drama and tension have gone from the project, as you all know by now that the car did get finished and did complete the Entente Cordial trip safely. Ah well, back to the tale of another restoration feature in retrospect. Lucky for me that I still have the ol' ball and chain around Paul Roach and with his help and encouragement we are getting the job done. Many a time he has pulled me from the corner of the garage screaming that I never want to see another Jaguar again.

There were more things to bolt on the bulkhead. On the driver's side went the pedal box with its new brake and clutch master cylinders along with the accelerator pedal. All were freshly cleaned and fitted with new bulkhead rubber gaskets supplied (along with the master cylinders) from the ever helpful Ray Ingman and Dick Bradley at Classic Spares. Then, using the parts book as my guide, I assembled the newly plated accelerator linkage and fitted it to the bulkhead. Use every source you can for reference as it avoids needless errors.

The servo vacuum tank was fitted to the lower bulkhead panel using a new one way valve. In the same position on the other side goes the servo itself. Bulkhead closing panels are fitted with new gaskets and the brake fluid reservoirs were made ready. These were extremely dirty from years of old fluid but they responded well to a good clean and were fitted to their respective sides of the bulkhead. The

Running at last. The engine and gearbox have been fitted and the air is full of delightful XK engine music.

The pedal box has been rebuilt with new master cylinders fitted. Here it receives its new bulkhead rubber gasket before being fitted.

rubber covers responded to a spring clean using thinners.

I was now able to fit the new brake pipes obtained from Automech. These wonderful pipes are easy to bend and come in the correct lengths clearly

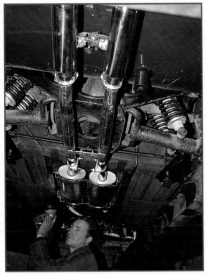

That's my third Double 'S' exhaust system to date with the one on the XK120 being nine years old now. This picture was taken a little later at the MoT bay as there is more room on their four-post ramp. We had great fun cleaning all that residual paint-shop dust and general restoration grime away after it was all finished.

marked as to what goes where. I had kept all the old pipes and used these as patterns to form the new pipe runs. The pre-formed shapes help to determine the correct location of the pipes along the frames. Being so pliable, a little tweak here and there is invaluable for those awkward corners.

The newly finished aluminium-sprayed manifolds looked a little bright and I wondered if I had made the right move but once they were on the engine I was to discover that they sobered a little, although they were still not to my taste. If there is someone out there who can produce the correct enamel finish that will stand regular use, please let me know. Fitting the Double 'S' exhaust was an untroubled operation. It is my third to date. I have been running one on my XK 120 for nine years without a problem and I have a system to eventually fit on my 'S' type saloon. I'm sold on the braided flexible joint on the down-pipes, always vulnerable on a Jaguar. The usual coil wrap relies so much on its own coil to keep it together. However, with the unique braided exterior, the whole joint is held in place giving superb protection. Realistically, two people are needed to hang the system, particularly when the car is resting on axle stands. A four post lift would be a huge help (dream on) but my newly installed pit proved its worth. Off the car, we loosely put all the components together just to make sure that the ends had not had a knock in transit. It is a credit to Double 'S' that the entire system arrived in the condition that it left the factory. Good packing certainly pays.

The two down-pipes went on first using new sealing rings and then loosely tightened to the manifold. As

These braided joints ('S' Type shown) are a unique feature on the Double 'S' exhausts ensuring that the usually vulnerable flexi-joint remains intact.

By arranging the exhaust clamps with the threads facing upwards, any chance of them bottoming over bumps or ramps is eliminated.

the centre box was quite heavy, we used a block of wood to provide some support while it was offered over the down-pipes. The four box support mounts had previously been fitted to the bodyshell and they lined up perfectly with the new silencer. These were fully tightened and eased the strain on the box. All we needed to do then was offer up the intermediate pipes and the rear chrome tail pipes. However, I had neglected to retain the little bridge bracket (the bracket is never a part of a replacement exhaust system) that holds the two tail pipes together and so we had a hurried search through the garage for an alternative. This duly sourced, the tail boxes could be mated together and secured on the rear bracket.

With the system hanging on its mounts, it was now time to tighten the exhaust clamps. The obvious thing to do is just have the clamps facing down. However, we are talking about an 'E' type here with low ground clearances. By giving a moment's thought, the clamps can be twisted through 180

It may look like a jumble in there but the torsion bar setting gauge (this one is adjustable) sits in the space vacated by the shock absorber.

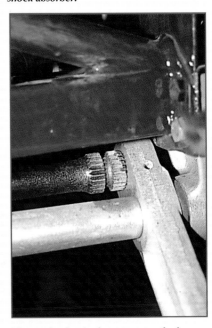

The torsion bar is about to enter the lower wishbone spline. Note the groove through the torsion bar spline, there to give clearance to the pinch bolt once in place.

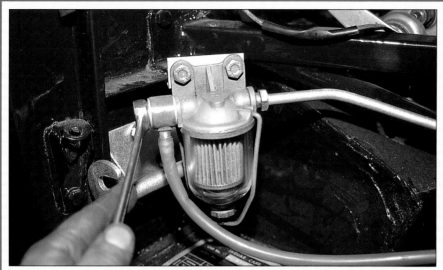

I always think that the fuel filter looks like an afterthought. There's a proper bracket but only one hole is used to secure it. The chassis plate was fitted first to get access for the rivets.

As the original header tank looked in good condition, we gave it a chance. The old style Kenlowe fan brackets are fitted on the mounting bolts.

All oils are topped-up and checked before starting the engine. The correct grade of oil for the carburettors is available from Burlen Fuel Systems.

degrees thus avoiding any chance scraping of the tarmac on bumps or ramps. From beneath the car, the new polished stainless steel exhaust looked terrific against the dark blue paintwork.

More than ever now I realise that I had made a mistake in not replacing the wiring loom. It will be done at a later date and I must admit that the job will be complicated by working on a fully built up car. We had a job remembering where the original loom ran. Looking at the books on originality only served to frustrate. What a complete waste of money they are. I found throughout the restoration that they would tell me nothing. On the contrary, the more I looked, the more inaccuracies I found. In the end, I simply referred to known original cars and followed their lead instead. The owner's handbook and the workshop manual did provide a few clues. Most wires fell into place with the oil pressure sender unit and rev-counter generator being obvious. I thought about replacing the oil pressure gauge with a mechanical unit as I have done many times in the past but opted to stay with the electrical system for convenience.

Next was the dreaded job of fitting the torsion bars. Actually, it's not as awful as it's made out. Each bar is

Wires running the wrong way around the ignition switch led to confusion when the engine failed to start. Not immediately apparent but obvious when discovered.

handed with a punched mark on the end. A splined muffler (not to be confused with the Americanism for exhaust silencer) secures it to the lower wishbone at the front and the reaction tie plate at the rear. To set it requires that the lower wishbone be free of all ties. So top ball joint, track rod end, shock absorber and roll bar are all disconnected, For the sake of convenience, a wire is strung between the suspension upright and the front

frame to stop the upright floundering around. A distance piece is inserted where the shock absorber once lived (full dimensions are given in the workshop manual). Our task was to fit the torsion bar so that both mufflers fitted their respective homes without having to use force or leverage to get the bolts in.

The reaction tie plate is fitted between the engine and gearbox. First, the torsion bar was passed through the reaction tie plate and then the front end offered up to the spline in the lower wishbone. This was rotated until the bolt holes were aligned. Then the rear muffler was slid on the rear splines and the bolt holes checked. They did not line up and so we had to keep rotating the torsion bar until they did. When we had it right, the torsion bar had to be driven home. Easier said than done. Using an old socket extension bar as a drift, the torsion bar edged its way along until it was fully home and we could put the pinch bolts into the lower wishbone and secure the bar. Finally, the suspension parts that we had dismantled were re-assembled.

I had thought to use the latest Kenlowe fan for the extra efficiency it gives but this involves removing a little of the original bracket so I stayed with the old style. The original Jaguar item I kept for an ornament. The existing radiator I knew to be reconditioned and the header tank looked good, so with a new set of hoses, the cooling system went together.

Now we were ready to fire up. All pipes and wires checked, ignition switched on. Nothing. The engine spun beautifully but it would not fire. When we fitted a live and earth lead straight to the coil from a separate battery, she started first time and what a blissful sound it was. The fault was eventually traced to the ignition/steering lock switch where the wiring had been run the wrong way round. With the ignition on, a live showed at the coil but when the key was turned to crank, all power was cut. Simple but extremely frustrating.

In the next issue, we start to fit the goodies and beautify our running car.

Acknowledgements in this issue go to Anglia Rustguard Ltd, Tel: 01376 344683; Automec Equipment & Parts Ltd, 36 Ballmoor, Buckingham MK18 1RQ, Tel 01280 822818; Burlen Fuel Systems, Tel 01277 412500; Double 'S' Exhaust Ltd Tel: 01884 33454; Classic Spares Ltd, Unit 4 Brook Road, Britannia Road, Waltham Cross, Herts EN8 7NP. Tel: 01992 716236 with a huge chummy 'ta mate' to Paul Roach.

BUILT 3000 MILES APART ON THE SAME FOUNDATIONS

In 1961 Jaguar made the parts that first put the E-Type on the road and SNG Barratt and British Auto USA are responsible for remanufacturing the parts that kept it there through the 1980's and the 1990's. Over the years our constant reinvestment in tooling to produce long obsolete parts has formed the core of the continuing commitment the SNG Barratt group have made to the Jaguar marque. Parts that we have made include the rev counter generator, indicator switches, dashboard switches, brake fluid bottle and sender unit, dash legend strip, handbrake warning light and headlight escutcheons, radiator cooling fan motors, bumpers and overriders, petrol sender units, fuel tank sludge filter, radiator header tanks, reproduction steering racks and many many more!!!!.

British Auto USA,
92 Londonderry Turnpike,
Manchester, New Hampshire 03104
Phone 603-622-1050 Fax 603-622-0849
E-mail jaguar@britishautousa.com

SNG Barratt Ltd,
The Heritage Building, Stourbridge Road,
Bridgnorth, Shropshire. WV15 6AP
Phone 01746-765432 Fax 01746-761144
E-mail barratt@barratt.co.uk

REGISTERED IN THE UK AS ISO9002 COMPLIANT THE FIRST IN OUR INDUSTRY

PROJECT E-TYPE

Taking shape, Jim Patten's 'E' type project is now on the home straight.

Angry? Yes, I was angry. Lured by false promises of excellence, I fell into the trap of handing the complete 'E' type brightwork over to a company unknown to me. With plenty of experience under my belt I should have known better. But the patter was impressive; plenty of good examples of previous work to inspect, a discourse on the techniques used plus an invitation to view the parts once the old chrome had been stripped off. Another bonus was they were in reasonable travelling distance from home, just through the Dartford tunnel.

I duly carried out my inspection using a felt tip as a schoolmaster would use the red pen highlighting those areas that 'could be better'. With the old chrome removed, I could see that there was virtually no serious pitting in the metal and the only ripples were caused by the chrome removal process. I was further impressed by another talk on how, once finished, the chrome should be taken straight to a heated area and thoroughly waxed as chrome was, by nature, porous. And on how the backs should be treated by a good primer and coated with the likes of Waxoyl. All good stuff so far. I made a point of asking after the welfare of the screen finishers and the door cappings during polishing but was told that these would present no problem. What could I say but "Make it so."

Completion dates came and went. Many a journey was wasted wearing my patience as thin as the metal on my bumpers would be by now. Eventually it was actually delivered to my home and what a mess it was. I could have strung a bow string on the door caps

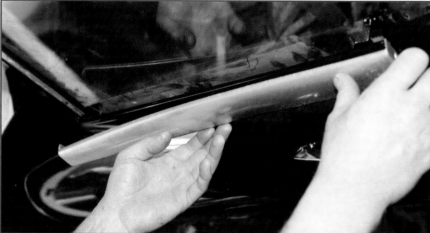

Irrepairable damage to the chrome door cap by a ham-fisted chroming company. Here, the re-plated part has been stripped again in an effort to get the shape back but it was impossible. See how badly it bows away from the door. It was replaced with a repro. part.

Original Dunlop brakes were used seen here (from above) prior to bleeding. It is important to get the brake pipes close to the caliper or they could rub against the wheel.

A single bolt holds the bonnet on each side where it runs in a nylon sleeved bush. Solid support was needed on the bonnet because it gets a bit unwieldy. Incidentally, those are JP's hands not Karen's, the bolt is just having a final tweak.

A flow of relief as the correct size alternator pulley is fitted. See how much larger the pulley is which was removed.

Hard-packed foam is being cut to size to provide an adequate seal between the heater and the bulkhead.

The wiper assembly proved simple to fit. The ball ends fit into the lever socket where 'ears' close down to seal the fit.

Before the dash-top is fitted the mirror stem base must go on first. It's probably easier to fit the stem at the same time. The dash-top is slotted and will fit around the stem.

they were so warped. The screen pillars had distorted into a 'U' bend and a couple of items for my XK120 were completely destroyed. We wrangled and argued but I refused to pay any more than the deposit I had left. I was left with no other option other than to buy reproduction parts which, in all fairness, proved to be pretty good. With excellent companies like Adam Howell around (see their ad in this issue), it seems crazy that I should have considered going elsewhere.

With the prevailing heat wave our conservatory was building up to a considerable temperature. What chrome we had accepted was left to simmer before working our polish into every chromed part. While still hot, the reverse (non-chromed) side of bumpers and overriders was painted with

Jenolite DoubleAct for protection. This would be followed up with a good dose of Waxoyl later. But the fitting of the chrome, door mechanism and trim will have to wait until the next issue.

Paul Roach and I were wondering at one point how we could dispose of this sleep thing; those extra wasted hours during the night would be invaluable now. The idea of uprating the brakes was shelved for a while as we decided to run standard to save precious time. On stripping the Dunlop brake calipers down we found them to be in superb condition. No corrosion, no wear lines, in fact they gave every indication of being fairly new. So, with a new overhaul kit, they were rebuilt and replaced along with new flexible hoses

to join the Automech brake pipes.

Ray Smith of Automech (01280 822818) and I had been in long conversation over the merits of silicone brake fluid. I had heard tales of soft pedals and all the other bar room myths. But I liked the idea of using a fluid that didn't absorb water at the rate a conventional fluid did. Making sure that all the brake components were of the latest specification, we gave it a go. Older brake parts and rubbers are not always compatible with modern brake fluids and this apparently, has given some credence to the old wives' tales about silicone fluid. That rear bleed nipple extension I had fitted to the rear brakes sometime earlier proved to be a tremendous idea. Trying to get at a regular 'E' type bleed nipple is about as rewarding as plucking a moonbeam from the sky. You can see both but getting your hands on them is another thing.

Starting with the wheel furthest away from the master cylinder, we worked our way around the car to the closest. Apart from a little difficulty in getting the fluid to the rear brakes, we had no trouble at all. I have spent days trying to get a decent pedal in the past. One time, all that squirted in the jar was more akin to bubbly when the cork is first pulled. The only way to get a firm pedal then was to bleed the system with the engine running. We did suffer the unusual problem of difficulty in bleeding the clutch however. Actually, the problem was related to the length of the push-rod, nothing to do with hydraulics at all. It did send the mind spinning for a while though. Being extremely tired it was hard to focus. Despite the fact that the parts book shows only a couple of push-rods, we found there to be several in reality. Mike Harris at LWR came to the rescue in the end. Being a smarty pants, he knows about these things. Ray Smith of Automech has been proved right about silicone brake fluid. The pedal is as firm as any pedal I have felt and, speaking retrospectively now, I can confirm that it performed well in action.

At last the bonnet could be fitted for keeps. This time we dragged Karen away from her Yoga session to pop the bonnet bolts in while Paul and I played a supporting role. The hinges had already been fitted and shimmed up, so it was only the two long end bolts with their sleeves to go on. Our newly-plated catches went on next with the internal levers temporarily fitted as we were still minus trim. It took a lot of fiddling to get the fit right because there are so many adjustments. Eventually we got it so that the bonnet closed equally on each side and the catches slid effortlessly into place.

Another problem to send us in a spin was fitting the alternator. Up to now it was just hanging in its cradle without the fan-belt fitted. It and the regulator unit fitted on the side of the bulkhead were easy enough to connect up as the loom was good enough for us to identify the colour of the wires. It was when we tried to fit the fan-belt that we thought we had the wrong one, as though the belt was not long enough. Checking with the old belt we still had the problem.

Thought to be a fiddly job turned out to be straightforward. These screen vent pipes just clip over the dash-top screen vents. Often, though, the pipes have collapsed at the ends and will need replacing.

The screen rubber provided is obviously from a saloon and needs cutting down to size. Here, Paul Roach works with the string buried inside the channel as the screen is eased into place. It was left to settle overnight before the rubber was finally cut.

In an effort to preserve the chrome, the backs of the bumpers and overriders are painted with Jenolite DoubleAct and finished with Waxoyl.

Rummaging through my bits and pieces, a longer belt was found but the alternator hit the side frame. We could do without these hold-ups. In desperation, we measured the alternator pulley. Having nothing to check it against, I called Henry Pearman. He confirmed the pulley to be too big and promptly posted a correct one off to me. I still owe him a replacement. Quite how the wrong pulley was fitted is beyond me.

By now the guide to originality book was laying in shreds on the floor. We intend to consign it to a ritual burning later. Putting the windscreen wiper mechanism in was not as difficult as anticipated. The connections are ball and socket type,

rather like large accelerator controls. However, when the motor was fitted it did not work. A quick dash across to Classic Spares (01992 716236) to bag a replacement took more time but at least they had one on the shelf. Four bolts hold this to the bulkhead with the many wires running into a block connector. We were in business. The heater box was one of the first lumps to be stripped way back. All the rusty parts were coated in Jenolite, primed and painted with black Smoothrite. I haven't got the frame of mind to powder coat everything black. Jaguar didn't, nor will I. This motor was tested first and now works perfectly on the car. New foam was used to seal the casing against the bulkhead. When the controls were connected to their new cables, all operated well.

Time to box the dash up. It looked so good and original that nothing was touched here. The clock had been forgotten so that will have to wait until later when I'll use the electronically modified type from Autoflux (01579 320459). A good blast with the air-line cleared away all the dust from inside while the dash and the dash top were cleaned with Armor All cleaner. I almost forgot to fit the mirror stem base as access is impossible once the dash top is on. The dash-top itself is easily secured on its brackets while the screen vent pipes are connected at the back.

I hadn't been looking forward to fitting the windscreen and thought about bringing in a specialist. Paul Roach talked me out of that. We had all the necessary parts via Classic Spares, screen rubber, top chrome screen retainer and lower chrome trim. The screen rubber was laid in place first and then the screen lowered down. However, the rubber channel had closed up and denied the screen entry. To counter this, we laid some string in the channel and, as the screen was lowered down, the string was pulled allowing the channel edges to slip around the glass. It was a gradual process, pulling on the string, pushing on the glass but we soon had it done. I had been warned that it was a mistake to trim the rubber surround too early as the weight of the screen can push the rubber still further down overnight. So, we weighted the screen and left it until the following day and yes, the screen had moved down. Now we felt it safe to trim the rubber. The top chrome was filled with a modern compound and pushed over the glass with the end caps securing it and the mirror stem fitted to the centre.

Completion of the project will be covered in Volume 8 No.4

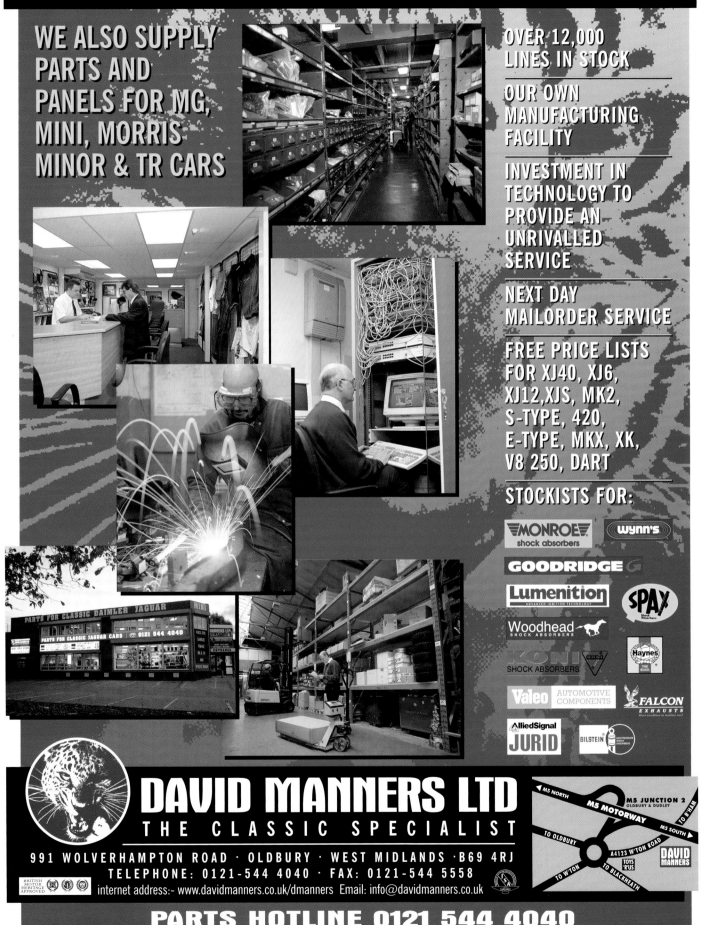

Looking magnificent, the 'E' type on its first outing to France.

PROJECT E-TYPE

It's finished!

Jim Patten celebrates by doing the Entente Cordial tour

The champagne corks were popping around the Patten garage as the 'E' type restoration was finally completed. All of those long days where my world was just four garage walls, finishing in the early hours of the morning, now seem worth while, although at the time we did wonder what on earth we were doing. Anglia TV got to hear of the project and how we were trying to meet an impossible deadline and take the car on the Entente Cordial tour. Intrigued, they decided it would make a worthy news item. So we had the company of the news team as the final parts went on the car. They returned on the morning we were pushing off to France and filmed us yet again driving up and down the local lanes. Needless to say, only a fraction appeared on Anglia News but it was good to get some media coverage for the trip.

It's a miserable feeling when you look at what seems a complete car with just a few jobs to go and yet the enormity of what is needed is really quite daunting. Stiff upper lip and all that, we got to it. What chroming we had received of an acceptable level could now be fitted. The bumpers and overriders actually looked OK. We had trial-fitted them before the body was sprayed. That meant, of course, that all of the captive bumper brackets were already fitted and caked with paint. Using a suitable tap, each thread was cleared prior to fitting the bumpers. Never try to force a bolt in. It may well work on the front but the rears are on a square plate that is simply pop-riveted to the body and will spin under pressure. A rubber seal fits around the edge of the bumper and is tucked under the bottom edge and held with a clip. The inside of the bumper and

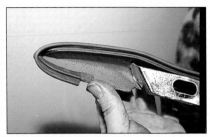
The inside of the bumpers had been fully protected with the rubber seal being fitted. Note the retaining clip on the bottom edge.

A tap was used to clear the paint-laden bumper mounts. A generous amount of Thread Guard will help to protect the thread in future.

An end stop in the bottom side window slide is positioned so that the window does not run to excess where it would be in danger of hitting the hood frame.

Those poor fingernails suffering as Karen fits the original trim to the new door panel. We had to make extra holes to accept the chrome strip.

overriders had been coated with Waxoyl and the bolts with Thread Guard. The whole front and rear assembly was fitted loosely at first to get the position right before finally tightening.

I was determined to fit the Nardi steering wheel but didn't like the centre horn push supplied with it. To get over this, I countersunk screws holding the rim to the boss as with the original and then had a sleeve made to take the Jaguar horn push. Then three holes were tapped in the side of the wheel boss so that retaining screws could be threaded in. I was really pleased with the result, except, of course, that the horn would not work when we tried it. The fault was traced to the horn relay. Not having another immediately available, the old one was opened up and the contacts cleaned. It seemed to do the job.

Karen meantime was trying to get years of grime out of the trim and seats. I am convinced that when a car is used regularly it can actually stay cleaner inside than one stored. Although our 'E' type had been dry stored, I suspect there must have been a lot of dust around. All of the trim had become ingrained with the stuff. Karen spent hours with a nail brush and proprietary cleaners trying to shift the dirt. Superficially it looks OK, but there still seems to be a congealed amount in the bottom of those tiny holes in the trim panels.

An order was placed with Creech (0181 659 4135) for the sill foam and window channel felt. Using the original sill covers as a pattern, the foam was cut to size and offered over the inner sill. All fitted well. Spray adhesive from 3M was used to fit the foam. Just the edges were glued on the outer cover because it is secured along the sill edge by a chrome strip. Now we could fit the 'A' post trim and permanently fix the bonnet catches. Using the original trim panels, we were able to use the existing screw holes.

I was very pleased with the reproduction chrome screen uprights; they seemed to fit reasonably well. The bottom screen chrome was fitted first although this did take a few attempts. Just as one part of the trim is pushed under the rubber lip, so another part popped up. Of course there is a special tool available but my kit does not extend that far. The screen uprights are tucked behind the screen rubber lip and pushed behind the screen pillar where they are pop-riveted in place. Naturally, the upright edge pops out of the rubber but it soon goes back. The screen top chrome rail is then placed over and screwed in place with the two endcaps. Our car has screen visors although I don't think they became standard until the Series 2. No matter, the fittings are placed under the screen end caps.

Then we looked at fitting the doors. At least the frames had been chromed well although only a small part protrudes. The channel felt comes in a roll. Adhesive was sprayed into the channel and then the felt is laid over the channel The side glass is pushed down forcing the felt into the channel. The glass was run up and down a couple of times to confirm the seating. When the adhesive dried, a sharp Stanley knife was used to trim the edges of the felt flush with the frame.

Each window winder mechanism was checked for operation and freshly greased. One securing screw had broken in its hole. This was drilled out and a new hole tapped in place. The door handles are fitted first with their section of the door locks. Working from above the door, the frame was lowered down in place. Then, being mindful of the small gap, the door glass followed. It is a bit tricky but, once the bottom winder guide passed through, all went well. Getting the winder mechanism and the door locks in was another period of frustration but perseverance won over. With everything in place, the various parts were screwed home. The winder mechanism has to be fitted to the door glass first. An end stop is fitted in the channel to stop the glass rising too high and hitting the hood frame. Ours was set too low so this will count as a later remedial job.

A sheet of clear plastic is laid across the inside door frame as protection before the door panel is fitted. The original backing board had warped quite badly and so new ones were obtained from Hutson's. These were a good fit but we had to make our own holes for the inner chrome strip. The existing trim fitted over OK and we had few problems putting the panel on the door. Chrome retaining strips hold the door panel in place but five are used on the leading edge of the door. Because the new panels were not shaped, they did need a bit of coercing to fit under the strips and on the bottom clips. By the time we had the handles and arm rest fitted, the panel was held firm.

Getting the centre console over the gear lever and handbrake provided great entertainment for the gathered

Just getting the headlamp scoop into the bonnet was tricky enough let alone getting the scoop fastened down.

Machining was required to get the Jaguar horn push to fit into the Nardi steering wheel but it was worth the effort. I consider this wheel to be much better than the original.

It's so easy if you're an expert. Bert Tyler fixes the number plate to the 'E' type bonnet using hot soapy water.

Finally, the 'E' type goes for its MoT and passes as should be expected. There were no flying colours as many boast. How can there be. It either passes or fails. It's not an examination where you get a grade.

assembly. I began to wonder if it actually came off the same car. Eventually it just slipped into place, I put the problem down to tiredness. The old carpets went back in as I didn't have time to source the correct type. A similar situation existed with the hood, although here the previous owner, Edward Vanderspar, had fitted a new top and it was still looking good. Sadly, only one door chrome cap could be located. A new weather strip was fitted but we would have to wait until we returned to fit the other side.

Moving forward to the bonnet, the wiring was placed inside the nose. I was lucky to have bought a new multi-connector some time earlier as the original had seen better times. The

headlamp scoops followed. They were a bit fiddly, particularly the rubber seal around the edge, but patience paid off. Once the light unit was in place the outer chrome surround could be fitted. Our old friends the chrome platers had been at work again as the rim had distorted. I was lucky to have the help of Paul Roach who is skilled in such manners and was able to get the shape back again. We had a real fight on our hands, though, when the rubber was tried. Somehow we couldn't get everything lined up. It didn't help that paint held the captive nuts firm. The threads had been cleared with a tap but the captives proved harder to loosen. Valuable time ticked away but we won through.

I was a bit concerned over the front number plate. My eye is fairly good but the sticky plate needed to be central on the bonnet. Bert Tyler of Appollo was coming over to carry out the final polish, so I persuaded him to do it. He amazed me by covering the bonnet with hot soapy water. To this he applied the number plate direct. It moved wherever he wanted it to, enabling the correct spot to be found with ease. His expert hands in the final polishing made the car look fabulous.

It's history now that the car made the trip. The MoT was a mere formality as it should be. But it was close. The test was on Thursday, we left for France on Friday. Foolish or supremely confident, take your choice. All I can say is that the 'E' type drives exactly as you would expect a new car to. It has that patina of a couple of years old car with that lovely original interior. We will be working to make that even more presentable in due course with replacement carpets and new hood following soon. I am still unsure about using chrome wire wheels. If only I could afford to keep a set for best. Whether I would take on such an intensive rebuild again, especially with the demands and deadlines associated with our type of work is another thing. All that matters now though is that I am truly delighted with the car. Acknowledgements to;

Alpha Autos, recovery (Tel: 0836 232114)
Anglia Rustguard (Tel: 01376 344683)
Appollo Autos, Coppen Road, off Selinas Lane, Dagenham, Essex RM8 1HJ (Tel: 0181 517 0926)
Brown Brothers, Coppen Road, Selinas Lane, Dagenham, Essex RM8 1QH (Tel: 0181 593 8811)
Classic Spares Ltd (Tel: 01992 716236)
Henry Pearman, Eagle 'E' Types (Tel: 01825 830966)
3M products available through trade motor factors.

THE HERITAGE LINE

PART 1
By Nigel Thorley

With the completion and handover of the Heritage XJ6 the Club have now taken on the next project for the Trust, a Series 3 "E" Type fixed head coupe. Work will begin with the assessment this month and in subsequent months the mechanical work will be 'attacked' by Dave Marks from David Marks Garages in Nottingham on behalf of the Club.

This particular car, registered WHP 205J, is the tenth fixed head made by the company and used extensively as a press car for road tests during 1971 and 1972. In fact, if any members have copies of the original *Autocar* and *Motor* magazines of the period (or even the Brooklands reprints) they will find this car has been featured many times.

Not too much is unfortunately known of the car's history except for the above. As will be noted throughout the refurbishment, there are a few 'non-standard' features and the car did lie at Jaguar's Browns Lane plant for a number of years mainly unused, the only telltale of use being the find of a petrol receipt dated January 8th 1976. It is also

thought that the car may have been used by some apprentices at some time and, in fact, in the eighties was partly retrimmed which included a new headlining.

The car has suffered the ravages of time despite the fact that at a distance it still looks reasonable and starts quite easily. The car has stood for a considerable length of time in less-than-ideal circumstances so corrosion has been aggravated, not only in the body but also in mechanical aspects, and we think that as time goes on the work involved will escalate.

BODILY

The bonnet is holed in several places and, although looking intact, will undoubtedly need a total replacement because, once the paint is removed, there is no doubt that the corrosion will have eaten deeper than origi-

nally suspected.

Some work has been done to the sill structure at some time, witness the extent of black undersealant coating, but nevertheless it is obvious that more sill to floor structural work will be required in due course. The doors are starting to blister at the bottoms and so will need remdial work if not reskins; again, only when they are stripped will the true extent of damage be revealed.

The rear wheelarches have rusted quite badly and have been unsuccessfully repaired (with filler) in the past. Some lamp units have been damaged, the 'V12' boot badge has been prised off and the under-structure has

The arrival and handover of the "E" Type to Dave Marks with Tony O'Keeffe of the JDHT on the left.

45

The only tell-tale of history left with the car was this fluid receipt found in the boot showing a modest £5 worth on January 8th 1976.

Re-trimmed in the boot, the floor is still sound.

The interior is overall in very good condition; note the lack of an oil pressure gauge – a mechanical one has been fitted to the engine bay in the past.

Although looking OK from a distance, the bonnet is holed in several places and the seams are starting to deteriorate.

A new headlining in the past is still in excellent condition, saving some work here.

Door bottoms are started to corrode, rubbers need replacing and panel fit is not that good.

Some re-upholstery has taken place which again eliminates work in this department.

been damaged (flattened) including air scoops which seem to indicate that the car has had a very hard life even to the point of transgressing off-road use at times!

The car has been painted previously and even touched-up since that time, all of which looks reasonable in photographs but in reality will necessitate a total repaint. The chrome is not bad, glass areas seem unscratched, probably all tyres will need replacement and the wheels rechromed.

MECHANICALLY

The car arrived at Dave Marks' premises running, although not on all cylinders and with the clutch slave cylinder completely seized which doesn't bode well for the remaining aspects of the hydraulic system. The brakes themselves work after a fashion but will obviously need a complete rebuild.

The engine has good oil pressure and

Rear wheelarches are filled but still deteriorating and there is lots of surface rust around the edges of every single panel.

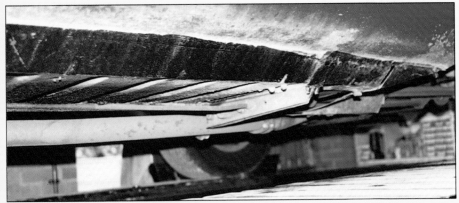

At some time the sills had had work carried out; witness the black undersealant but here again deterioration is still taking place.

At the rear lots of hardened mud have aggravated the bodywork condition and the exhaust has rusted out.

Light units like this offside rear will need replacement.

Underneath air scoops have been flattened and broken and the hardened mud pushed into crevices seems to indicate some attempt at grass-track racing!

More rust and some damage to the subframe here from grounding.

Although a steam-clean helped to 'find' everything under the bonnet, there are large expanses of corrosion around ancillaries.

A good example of the rusting of ancillary parts due to damp storage.

sounds sweet but has a chronic fuel starvation problem. Replacing the in-line filter made no difference so a complete refurbishment of the fuel system, carburation, etc. will be in order. It should be noted that the engine has been 'played' with by various people with evidence of test rigs and, in fact, is NOT the original unit that should be with the car. It is not known why the engine was changed and now the car features an early XJS unit.

Severe corrosion of the waterways has taken place and the hoses will need to be replaced; even the radiator appears in very bad condition. The exhaust system has collapsed and part of the rear pipes are missing and many ancillary components will require cleaning and powder-coating.

STRATEGY

Dave's strategy on the mechanical side is first to remove the engine/gearbox assembly from the car. Then to dismantle the front and rear subframes and other mechanical ancillaries so that everything can be worked on separately away from the bodyshell. Both subframes will then be stripped, evaluated and rebuilt with all new parts; ancillaries will be cleaned off, repaired, replaced and/or repainted as required.

The engine seems to have covered a low mileage and, in fact, the speedometer reads 9,000 miles which seems to indicate that this was changed at the same time as the engine although there is no written evidence to substantiate this. As such, Dave plans to clean and flush it out and effectively bench-test it for compression, etc. in the hope of not having to strip it down. To date, although not running on all cylinders, the engine sounds smooth with no knocks or smoke.

Next month we will cover the removal of engine and gearbox.

An example of 'extra' equipment on this factory car is this secondary oil pressure sender unit that plugs into the front of block, perhaps to establish oil pressure along the length of the crankshaft.

THE HERITAGE LINE

PART 2

By Nigel Thorley

This month Nigel Thorley reports on the start of work in earnest by Dave Marks on the Jaguar Daimler Heritage Trust "E" Type Series 3 with the removal of the engine and gearbox from the car.

TRIM REMOVAL

It is necessary to remove the central console interior trim to gain access to allow the removal of the engine/gearbox from the car. The radio console is held in place at the bottom by two 7/16in chrome nuts (*à la* XK engine rocker cover!), one per side of the console. Two other knurled chromium fasteners are also removed at the top sides of the panel. Disconnecting the two cigar lighter connections then allows the console to be withdrawn from the car. No radio was fitted to this car but, had there been, of course this would have to be disconnected as well.

To remove the main console running between the seats necessitates removal of the ashtray and undoing four Phillips head screws which permits the console to be lifted over the handbrake assembly. With the console completely removed and stored safely as it had been re-upholstered not that long ago, access was gained to the gaiter surrounding the gearlever, held in place by six Phillips head screws. With this undone and removed, the pin that secures the gearlever in place is exposed. Once the gearbox mounting is undone and the box dropped slightly, this pin will become more accessible for removal without the necessity to remove the interior gearbox surround.

In our case the centre console was easily removed because there was no radio to disconnect.

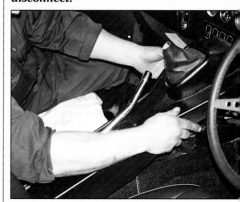

The long console base has to be lifted up and forward to clear the handbrake assembly to remove.

With the consoles out, access is gained to the Phillips head screws that hold the gearlever gaiter in place.

The pin securing the gearlever in place is accessible but not removable at this stage without lowering and supporting the gearbox once the mounting has been undone.

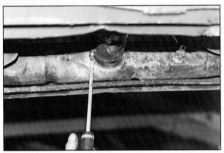

Corrosion around the radiator with much more corrosion coming to light once the hoses were removed.

Lots of corrosion throughout the cooling system will necessitate further investigation in the engine later. Note the slight bodywork damage underneath the car caused by grounding at some time.

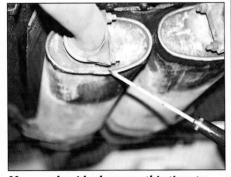

More underside damage, this time to the exhaust system with build-up of mud which would seem to indicate the car has been driven at speed over bumpy grassed areas in the past!

UNDERSIDE WORK

After draining the cooling system, which in this case was sadly lacking anti-freeze to protect against internal corrosion, all the hoses were disconnected, most of which were

The exhaust system off the car and not salvagable.

rearward, most of which was totally unserviceable and will necessitate complete replacement later. The removal involved burning off the bolts. The downpipes remained *in situ*, coming out with the engine/gearbox assembly.

The four bolts securing the propshaft to the gearbox were removed and the exact position of the propshaft in relation to the output shaft of the gearbox was marked with the aid of a centre-punch. As mentioned before, this ensures the correct re-alignment and therefore balance upon reassembly.

The rear gearbox mounting was then removed and the gearbox supported to prevent the weight resting on the bulkhead. Dropping the gearbox just slightly allowed the pin securing the gearlever to be removed (as mentioned earlier), subsequently allowing

With the gearbox mounting undone the gearbox was supported while the engine was prepared for removal.

The radiator came out as a complete unit with electric fans.

unserviceable as were the Jubilee clips retaining them in place. The lack of anti-freeze had caused even the pipe unions to corrode and, until further stripdown of the engine, the full consequences of this lack of corrosion inhibitor are unknown.

While underneath the car Dave removed the exhaust system from the downpipes

the lever itself to be withdrawn. The speedometer cable was undone, the drive being located aft of the rear gearbox extension housing. The knurled ring unscrewed, releasing the speedometer cable.

Disconnecting the clutch operating mechanism normally involves removing the flexible hose. In this case the hose was badly

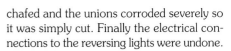

Header tank removal revealing more corrosion through lack of anti-freeze.

Removing tie-bars from underneath the engine compartment; note the slight bend (damage from an earlier incident!).

Undoing rear engine mounting on the driver's side necessitates access from inside the car.

Although not absolutely necessary, the removal of the alternator and bracketry help prevent possible damage when removing the engine from the car.

chafed and the unions corroded severely so it was simply cut. Finally the electrical connections to the reversing lights were undone.

ENGINE BAY WORK

Back on top of the car in the engine bay the throttle and choke cables were removed. Each choke cable is held in place by a spring clip to the carburettor body and attached to the choke spindle by a 1/4in AF pinch bolt. Prising off the clip and unscrewing the pinch bolt releases it. The throttle cable is disconnected simply by undoing a 1/2in AF lock nut, withdrawing the cable off the capstan housing and disconnecting it from the capstan.

The main engine wiring loom meets up to the body loom by a six-pin block connector and two separate single-wire connectors. Separating these and removing the main battery feed to the starter motor and alternator connections will isolate the wiring from the engine.

The radiator needed to come out and was removed by undoing two 9/16in AF nuts at the base and two 7/16in AF nuts holding the radiator to its top brackets. The radiator is lifted out complete with its cooling fans so again all wiring connections had to be separated.

The engine frame cross-brace was also removed by undoing the three 9/16in AF nuts and bolts each side which also secure the fresh air vent brackets (which incidentally are a retro-fit to this particular V12 "E" Type, only fitted to later models). These bolts also keep in place the air trumpet supports. The cross-brace is removed along with the

Left: Dave Marks (with back to camera) being assisted in the removal of the "E" Type engine by Brian Reid.

Below: Getting the angle of lift is important to ensure the engine and transmission clear the bulkhead.

50

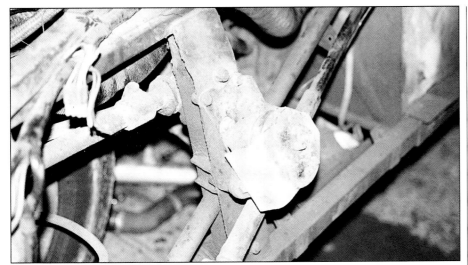

of the Club) the lifting began by Dave while Brian kept a keen eye on the movement, particularly noting that the engine/transmission was not fouling the bulkhead or other parts of the car.

The 'lump' has for the moment been put to one side pending more dismantling on the car.

NEXT MONTH
Next month Dave starts work on removing the front and rear subframes, relieving the shell ready for remedial bodywork.

With the engine out, note the squashed engine mounting which will necessitate replacement.

radiator header tank.

For reasons of manoeuvrability and the maximum reduction of risk to the alternator and its bracketry, these were removed by undoing the adjusting brackets' 9/16in AF nuts and bolts, removing the fan belt and noting the position of all the spacers fitted.

UNDERNEATH – TAKE 2
Back underneath the car the engine frame front cross-bar ties held on by 9/16in AF nuts either end were also removed. Another cross-bar is situated underneath the rear of the engine and is accessed from the footwell

inside the car via two (one each side) 3/4in bolts.

The nearside engine mounting is accessed from the top via a single 9/16in AF nut between the suspension bars, the offside one accessed from underneath via a hole in the wheelarch dustshield.

ENGINE OUT TIME
With all umbilicals released it was now time to remove the massive V12 lump from the "E" Type. With the aid of appropriate lifting tackle and another body (in this case Brian Reid from the Coventry and Hinckley region

Engine out, next month suspensions out.

THE HERITAGE LINE

PART 3

By Nigel Thorley

This month Nigel Thorley covers the removal of front and rear subframes with David Marks.

JAGUAR-DAIMLER HERITAGE TRUST "E" TYPE REFURBISHMENT

Regular readers will already have seen the removal of the engine and gearbox assembly from the car last month. This month the stripdown continues with the removal of all other mechanical aspects, effectively leaving a 'clean' bodyshell which will be transported away for remedial bodywork to be featured in later articles in this series.

REAR AXLE REMOVAL

The first task was to drain off the rear axle oil by undoing the 1/2in square drive plug underneath the differential. The oil was drained off into a container to examine its condition which revealed that the car had lacked regular attention and the amount of silvered colour and debris was indicative of bearing wear so inevitably the axle will need stripping down (to be covered later in the refurbishment).

The wheels were undone and removed with support under the subframe which also allowed the six bolts and four nuts (1/2in AF) per side holding the subframe to the rubber 'V' mounts to be removed. After this and inside the car under the rear carpet were the two (per side) 1/2in AF bolt heads which,

Dave completed the subframe removal on his ramp which permitted the use of professional jacking equipment to support the car and when the shell was free would ease the removal to a flat-bed trailer.

when undone, allow the removal of the radius arm securing straps. Lastly, in this area the 5/8in AF bolt securing the radius arm to the body was undone which then allowed the arm to drop free on each side. (Normally the arms have to be sprung loose from the body but in the "E" Type's case they just fell away).

Returning to the 1/2in bolts that secured the radius arm securing straps, one of these

Pulling back the carpet in the rear footwell reveals the two 1/2in bolts securing the radius arm securing straps to the body.

bolts has a double purpose in that it also holds the rear brake air scoop in place. To enable the scoop to be removed totally, however, it is also necessary to remove the two Phillips-head self-tapping screws securing the scoop to the chassis. One of the scoops was perfectly serviceable; the other

Removing the Phillips-head screws that secure the brake air scoops to the chassis.

Dave undoing the 1/2in plug to drain off the old differential oil before dismantling the completely subframe from the "E" Type.

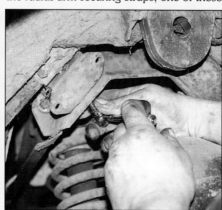

Removing the 1/2in nuts holding the subframe 'V' mountings to the body.

Centre-popping the position of the prop-shaft universal joint in relation to the differential output shaft so that the two can be realigned in the same position upon reassembly.

The released propshaft can be withdrawn from the front of the car with ease while the rear subframe is still in situ.

ing out the work on his ramp the next task was to support the body via the rear cross-member on a transmission jack high enough to allow the subframe to be completely removed.

Lastly, before starting work on the front of the car, Dave opted to remove the rear heat shield panel by drilling out the pop rivets. This saves another job when the bodywork is started later.

FRONT AXLE REMOVAL

Turning attention to the front of the car, Dave continued to work with the body *in situ* on the ramp. This meant supporting the rear of the bodywork securely with wooden sleepers before starting because, as the weight of the car was lightened at the front, so there might have been a tendency for the body to tip rearwards if not adequately supported.

The first task as before was to remove the front wheels after supporting the front of the body underneath the torsion bar reaction brackets.

Next off came the brake calipers. The locking wires on 5/8in AF bolts were removed and the bolts were then undone, so freeing the calipers. Next undoing the brake pipes where they entered the calipers caused problems because the pipes twisted with the turning of the nut (these will have to be replaced anyway). The calipers were then removed from the car.

At this stage both the brake discs and brake pads were found to have virtually no wear on them whatsoever although, because of the length of time the car has been stand-

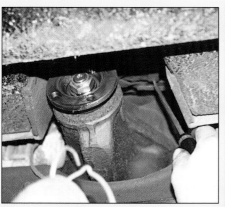

Weeping oil all around the differential output shaft indicated seal problems.

as mentioned in a previous article has been flattened so will need replacement. Next came the removal of the propshaft where it connects to the output shaft flange of the differential. First it is normal to mark the exact relationship for reconnection to ensure the correct balance. Dave always suggests this is done by a centre-punch. The propshaft is disconnected via four 9/16in AF nuts and bolts. With this done the propshaft was removed from the front (as it had previously been disconnected from the gearbox end as mentioned last month).

An aside here was that some oil was weeping from the output shaft of the differential which indicates seal replacement will be necessary.

An often forgotten item, the removal of the grease nipples to avoid damage when the rear subframe is removed.

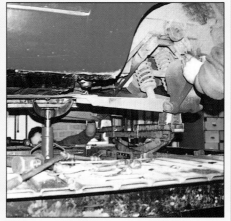

There is no substitute for adequate support when carrying out an operation like this. In Dave's case and using the jacking system built into his ramp he also supported the body via a transmission jack.

With the subframe released from the car, the ramp was lowered, bringing with it the subframe while the transmission jack continued to support the bodyshell.

Next off came the handbrake cable by undoing the R-clip which acts as the retainer for the clevis pin, then pushing the pin up disconnecting the cable from the operating linkage. Then, undoing the 11/16in AF locknut, the cable was screwed out of the adjuster and fully withdrawn. The brake flexi-hoses were in a terrible condition and will obviously need replacement so for ease of removal Dave just cut through them!

The rear subframe was now effectively completely free of the body and the last job was to remove the hub grease nipples (3/8in AF spanner) to avoid damage should the subframe drop to the floor. With Dave carry-

Drilling out the rivets holding the rear heat shield on to the bodywork.

As the brake pipe securing nuts were undone, so the pipes began to twist out of shape confirming their replacement will be necessary upon reassembly.

Removing the discs and hubs intact for work later.

Calipers now off the car, Dave Marks noting the excellent condition of the discs which appear hardly to have been used since fitted.

ing (in not the best of conditions), deterioration is such that they will unfortunatley have to be replaced anyway!

The next stage was to remove the discs themselves. Prising off the dust cap, removing the split pin and castellated nut allowed the discs and hub assemblies to be withdrawn for later work.

Next Month:

Next month we see Dave continue with the stripdown which involved the removal of the stub axles, steering rack and all ancillaries and the eventual transportation of the empty bodyshell off site for later attention.

THE HERITAGE LINE

PART 4

By Nigel Thorley

The continuing strip-down of the Jaguar-Daimler Heritage Trust Series 3 "E" Type by Dave Marks covered by Nigel Thorley.

JAGUAR-DAIMLER HERITAGE TRUST "E" TYPE REFURBISHMENT

STUB AXLE REMOVAL

After the work completed last month, this time Dave starts off with the removal of the stub axles and, with the aid of a 3/4in AF spanner, the top ball joints were undone and split with the aid of the proper equipment. The ball joint gaiters were found to be degraded but again these would need replacement anway.

A 3/4in AF nut released the steering track rod ends after which the bottom ball

Undoing the top ball joints with a 3/4in AF spanner.

joints were also split. The stub axles were then removed from the car. At this stage the shock absorbers were retaining the force of the torsion bar on its full extension.

The anti-roll bar was separated from the

other wishbone by undoing the 5/8in-headed bolt and its 11/16in nut. The bolt holding the anti-roll bar on to the drop arm was also

Using a splitter on the "E" Type's ball joints.

Note the degraded state of the rubbers.

Stub axle removed from the "E" Type.

removed. A bottle jack was placed underneath the lower wishbone in an attempt to take weight off the torsion bar to allow the shock absorber to be removed safely. Due to the fact that so many parts had been removed from the car up to this time including the engine, there wasn't really sufficient weight to remove the shock absorbers easily.

First, the split pins holding the castellated nuts on to both the top and bottom shock absorber pins were seized so at this stage the nuts were simply undone and the remains of

Removal of the anti-roll bar.

the pins will be drilled out at a later date. Then, with the jack under the torsion bar, the top bolt had to be drifted out due to the tension created by the torsion bar. Once the shock absorber was off at the top it slid easily off the lower bolt and was discarded as new ones will be fitted upon reassembly.

Next off came the fresh air ducting to give ease of access, this being held on by Jubilee clips and cable ties. Cable ties also secured the screen wash tubing which was also removed.

The engine mounts were undone and removed, giving access to the top wish-

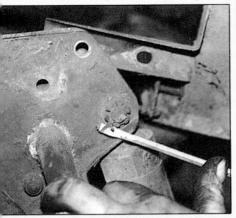

Removing the castellated nut split pin from the top shock absorber mounting.

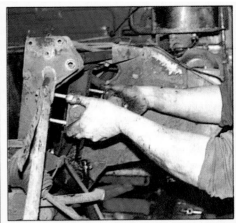

bolts. A 1/2in AF nut and bolt secure the universally jointed steering column connection to the rack. The unions securing the power steering entry and return pipes have to be disconnected from the rack along with the fluid return pipes to the pinion. This enabled the pinion to clear the engine frame.

The rack can then be withdrawn from the car. The steering rack mountings are held on to the frame by one locknut per side which allows these to be withdrawn free of the car. It should be noted that it is important for safety reasons that "E" Type steering rack mountings are assembled correctly and this will be covered in detail in a later article.

Above and below: Torsion bar removal

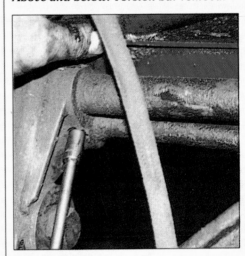

Removal of ducting and cables clearing the engine bay of as much as possible.

bones. When the bushes are removed there are shims which must be kept in the same quantity and order for reassembly to give a basis for final adjustment.

TORSION BAR REMOVAL

The next stage was to remove the torsion bars. From underneath the 11/16in AF nuts and bolts holding the torsion bar to the reaction plate were undone and removed and the longer 5/16in nut and bolt acting as a locking screw at the front lower wishbone mount were removed. Dave then attempted to drift out the torsion bar. Unfortunately these were seized into position and so a second method of attack was attempted. By undoing the two 9/16in bolts holding the front wishbone mountings to the engine frame and undoing the 11/16in castellated nut securing the wishbone pin to the rear mount, Dave was then able to drift out the wishbone and torsion bar assembly complete from the car. This then exposed the lower bolt on the rear wishbone mount which, along with the upper, was then removed and the bracket stored for safety.

Two 1/2in AF nuts and bolts either side secure the anti-roll bar to the front frame, these also securing the horn mounting points which can then be removed after disconnecting the electrical connections.

STEERING RACK REMOVAL

With the anti-roll bar removed access is gained to the bottom steering rack securing

ANCILLARIES

With hubs, discs, steering, etc. removed it was also necessary to relieve the bodywork of everything else that would affect remedial bodywork to be carried out.

The splash panels behind the front wheels to the sills were undone and, although in a semi-reasonable state, will also be replaced later. The screenwash reservoir was unscrewed and removed.

Returning to the splash panels, the brake servo reservoir was also secured to the nearside and was undone, the electrical connections released and the body taken out. The vacuum reservoir was held on to the sill by a 7/16in AF bolt and to the splash panel. The three vacuum pipes were cut free (again due for replacement), one to the servo, one to the master cylinder and one to the engine.

The brake servo itself was secured from inside the car via the nearside bulkhead by three nuts. Brake lines were disconnected (again total replacement will be carried out upon reassembly), the 7/16in AF union between the master cylinder and servo was disconnected and the 7/16in nut and bolt securing the bracket for the servo to the engine frame was also removed. The servo, with a struggle, does manipulate through the A frames.

Next out came the heater box simply bolted to the bulkhead by 1/2in AF bolts and saddle clamp to the A frame. With the pipes disconnected and the operating cables disconnected this was removed, revealing

Disconnecting the horn connections.

Pulling back the carpet in the passenger's foot well reveals the three nuts that secure the brake servo in position.

Removal of the brake servo is a manipulation process through the front frame.

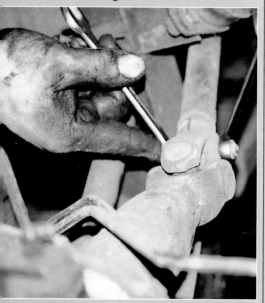
Disconnecting the universally mounted steering column from the rack.

The severe corrosion underneath the heater box, only revealed when off the car.

extensive corrosion to the underside.

The flexible fuel line was removed from the rigid fuel lines. Two Phillips head screws secured the screenwash pump to the bulkhead which was also removed, one screw of which was also the earth point.

The wiring harness was disconnected from its securing ties around the frames and pushed through the bulkhead out of the way. The harness at the front of the car is secured to the frame which also needed disconnecting.

Disconnecting the wiper motor electrical connections the motor itself is secured to the bulkhead by four 1/2in AF bolts and, when undone, the drive to the rack can be disconnected via a 7/16in nut, leaving the rack completely *in situ*. The two bulkhead mounted ignition and starter relays are also removed, held in position by 5/16in AF bolts.

The pedal box is secured to the bulkhead via five 1/2in AF nuts, accesssed from inside the driver's footwell. Removing these allowed the box to be withdrawn through the A frame. Lastly, the altenator regulator was secured via 5/16in AF bolts; when undone and the electrical connections removed, this was also withdrawn.

Screen wash pump secured to the bulkhead also acting as an earth point.

As can be seen from the accompanying photographs, the stripdown is now complete, since when the bodyshell has been removed and details of this will appear in subsequent future issues.

For the moment, however, Dave Marks will set to work dismantling the various mechanical aspects to evaluate new parts required. This will be covered in next month's article.

After some fiddling the rack finally comes away from the car.

THE HERITAGE LINE

PART 5

By Nigel Thorley

JAGUAR-DAIMLER HERITAGE TRUST "E" TYPE REFURBISHMENT

The shell 'clean' of mechanicals as it arrived from David Marks to Renascence Cars in Atherstone.

The same frontal aspect with glass removed and the start of paint removal.

This month Nigel Thorley gives Dave Marks a break from the mechanical aspects and turns his attentions to the bodywork.

The extremely good condition of the shell under the bulkhead.

As regular readers will have noted, Dave Marks stripped out all mechanical aspects of the bodyshell so that it could then be removed to another site for remedial work and for this project the car has been moved to Tom Priestnall's Renascence Cars in Atherstone, near Nuneaton, just off the M42 motorway.

Renascence Cars are well-known for their race preparation and restoration work on all manner of Jaguars from original racers from the fifties to the very latest XJs and a full report on the company can be read in next month's Specialist feature within *Jaguar Enthusiast*.

For now, though, let's take a look at what Tom has done so far with the Heritage "E" Type Series 3 fixed head coupe.

Again, as regular readers may have noted, our initial impression of the "E" Type bodyshell was one of sad neglect to the point where the maroon paintwork had oxidised badly, some underbody damage had been noted and, at first glance, large areas of rust would reveal major corrosion problems. However, as things have turned out, this couldn't have been further from the truth.

The Heritage "E" Type is a prime example of how difficult it is to assess how severe bodywork problems are until you actually get the paint stripped off.

The first task at Renascence was to remove most of the interior trim to avoid any unnecessary damage and at the same time

Trim removal to prevent unnecessary damage.

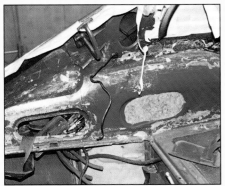

Underneath the trim; everything looks in excellent order.

Minor surface rusting in the boot well is no problem.

Small amount of corrosion in driver's footwell...

...but hardly anything on passenger side.

Again, by no means severe corrosion around the door/sill closing areas.

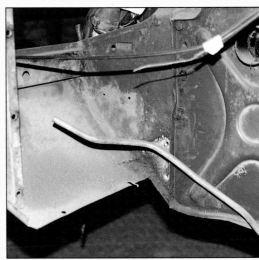

Top & Above: Forward sill inner areas show slight rusting but once cleaned up with the heat gun and sander, again no major concern.

A little more severe on the rear inner wheelarch edges but again not sufficient to warrant new panelling.

to give good access to the inside of the body panels to assess repairs further. The trim has been safely stored until needed and full information on this will be published when it is reassembled once the bodywork/paintwork is complete.

Next out came the glass and remains of chrome trim, door handles, etc. and the complete removal of the two doors, tailgate and front frames from the bodyshell. The wiring loom has been retained but strapped up out of harm's way and the dashboard area has been protected.

Next, every panel on the bodyshell has been hand stripped of paintwork by a combination of heat gun and abrasive sander as this is the only way to get back to absolutely clean bright metal to analyse exactly how far

The tailgate during stripppping, again in remarkable overall condition.

Again other small areas requiring remedial work where the rear bumpers connect to the wings/valance area.

Before and after – front frames, one cleaned, the other about to be – no problems again here.

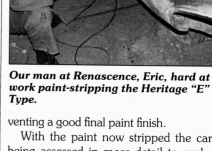

Our man at Renascence, Eric, hard at work paint-stripping the Heritage "E" Type.

One of the doors removed from the car and partly stripped showing no signs of major corrosion either.

Seamed edges of doors will require some work.

any corrosion has gone. Other methods like shot-blasting would have been preferable but would have meant completely stripping every last nut and bolt from the car which wasn't felt necessary for this refurbishment; or alternatively chemical paint removers which Renascence, like many other specialists, have now outlawed because of the possibility of contamination to other vehicles or the likelihood of retention on the metal pre-

venting a good final paint finish.

With the paint now stripped the car is being assessed in more detail to evaluate how far to go with bodywork repairs. It certainly appears that the bodyshell is in far better condition than originally anticipated and therefore it is a pity to consider many new panels.

A full report on the outcome and the next stage of proceedings will be covered in next month's article. In the meantime let the pictures speak for themselves on the condition of the Jaguar-Daimler Heritage Trust V12 "E" Type.

The bodyshell virtually stripped ready for a complete reappraisal of the remedial work necessary.

THE HERITAGE LINE

PART 6

By Nigel Thorley

As the general principles of the independent rear suspension stripdown have been covered in recent articles on the JDHT XJ6 refurbishment, this time we cover the detail more in pictures than text:-

Removal of the rear subframe base plate, undoing 6" AF nuts and bolts and 8" AF bolts.

The excellent condition of the base plate showed no signs of jacking marks, etc. so will be cleaned up and powder coated.

This month Nigel Thorley returns to David Marks Garage in Nottingham to cover the stripdown of the rear suspenson subframe of the Jaguar-Daimler Heritage Trust "E" Type Series 3 fixed head coupe.

Removing the shock absorber pins 11/16"AF socket size.

Extracting the pins with the aid of a plastic headed mallet to prevent unnecessary damage.

Pushing the front shock absorber out of the way slightly allows the special 3/4" AF flat-sided bolt to be removed that holds the radius arm onto the hub. The arms will also be cleaned up and powder coated before refitment.

Removing the split-pins holding the hubs on to the half-shafts.

Undoing the 1 1/8" AF bolt securing the hub.

After attaching a hub puller by means of the car's own road wheel nuts, the puller's thread is screwed in to react against the half-shaft after which the shock of hammer action against the puller allows the hub to extract.

Removing the 15/16" AF nut securing the outer fulcrum pin in place.

Extracting the outer fulcrum pin which is normally relatively easily removed.

The inner fulcrum pin is held in place by a 3/4" AF nut which when removed.....

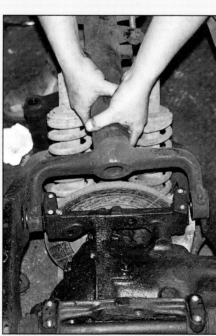

..... allows the lower wishbone to be removed along with all its washers and seals, all of which will be replaced.

Removing the four 11/16" AF half shaft to disc bolts.

When removing the half-shaft it is vital to take note of the shim positions as these must be returned to the same position upon reassembly.

One of the hubs would not extract from the half-shaft so the use of Dave's press came handy, nevertheless vital to ensure an even loading so as not to damage the castellations.

This shows the relatively 'dry' condition of the half-shaft universal coupling indicating poor greasing in the past.

The al- important distance shim to get the correct bearing pre-load; this will be taped to the half-shaft for safe keeping.

Dave Marks centre-spotted all sided components to ensure correct reassembly at a later date. In this case two punch marks indicated offside components.

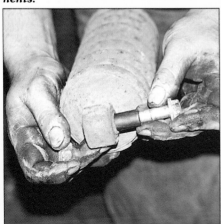

An 11/16" AF nut and 5/8" AF bolt head will undo the shock absorbers from the frame, not forgetting to retain the spacer in the top shock abosorber bush.

To assist in the removal of the differential it is advisable to undo the screw-threaded breather housing stem to prevent it getting damaged.

Removing the handbrake balance mechanism from the cage held in place by two 1/2" AF bolts to the top.

Cutting the lock wire from the main differential to cage securing bolts.

Four special 3/4" AF bolts secure the differential to the cage. These are not reused but discarded and replaced upon reassembly with new.

Undoing the brake pipes to caliper connections. The old pipes are kept as patterns to make up the correct length and bend on the new pipes.

The cage being removed from the differential and brake assembly.

Removing the split-pins securing the compensators to each caliper.

Condition of the compensators was excellent, only requiring cleaning before reassembly.

After cutting the locking wire from the calipers allowing the 5/8" AF bolts to be removed to free them from the differential.

The removed calipers and handbrake calipers will be split down and refurbished at a later date.

Next sliding the discs free from the differential output shafts more shims are revealed which must also be retained in their exact position for reassembly.

Removing the inner fulcrum pin protective sleeve which will be claned up for reuse.

Cutting more lock wires the 11/16" AF bolts are undone allowing the differential yokes to be removed. These bolts and the appropriate shims will all be replaced upon reassembly.

The rear brake discs look as if they had been replaced prior to the "E" Type being laid up some years in the past. However, due to corrosion they will now have to be replaced again!

That completes the stripdown of the rear subframe of the JDHT "E" Type. In the next article Dave starts the mammoth task of stripping down the ancillaries from the V12 engine to evaluate its overall condition. Meanwhile Renascence continue to prepare the bodyshell for remedial work and new panels; more on this in a future issue.

The differential casing free ready for cursory inspection and cleaning. Note the shims retained securely in position.

THE HERITAGE LINE

PART 7

By Nigel Thorley

This month Nigel Thorley relates the stripdown of engine/gearbox from the Jaguar-Daimler Heritage Trust's Series 3 "E" Type, being mechanically prepared by David Marks' garage in Nottingham.

JAGUAR-DAIMLER HERITAGE TRUST "E" TYPE REFURBISHMENT

As regular readers will already know, the engine/gearbox assembly has been removed from the bodyshell and, up to now, has been stored awaiting stripdown and inspection. For safety reasons and to provide an easier working environment, Dave mounted the engine on a specially-designed stand but prior to this the head shields from the top of the engine were removed to prevent damage (a common problem on Series 3 "E" Type engines).

Removing the engine head shields held in place by two 7/16 AF nuts on each shield.

GEARBOX REMOVAL

A further job prior to fitting the engine securely to its stand was to disconnect the gearbox.

Four 7/16 AF bolts secure the bottom gearbox plate.

The bottom gearbox plate removed.

Two 9/16 AF bolts secure the starter motor in place which also needs to be removed. Note the second bolt also secures the clutch hydraulic pipe. The starter can then be withdrawn which will be sent away for refurbishment.

A further seven 9/16 AF bolts are loosened which secure the bellhousing to the engine. The top two are initially retained in situ to provide support to the gearbox/bellhousing until ready to remove.

One of the top bolts also secures the engine breather in position.

At this point the engine is still supported on a hoist which is lowered almost to the ground allowing the gearbox/bellhousing to be removed without letting it drop too far.

Looking inside the bellhousing revealed no 'nasties' – eg. oil leaks, etc.

CLUTCH REMOVAL

Six 9/16 AF bolts hold the clutch plate in place which is also removed.

The clutch, although in reasonable condition, will be replaced.

With the clutch removed, the flywheel is visible. It was in excellent condition.

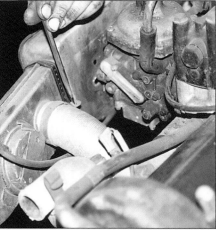

Phillips-head screws hold the amplifier in position which is also removed, noting again more spacers.

At this stage the 7/8in sump plug is removed, allowing the oil to be completely drained from the engine. This will allow the engine to be turned when on the stand without the fear of losing fluid and creating its own mess!

There are over 2½ gallons of oil in a V12 engine and this container would normally be sufficiently deep to accommodate that amount. However, the oil in this engine has been severely diluted by petrol, probably by constant cold start/stop driving.

Undoing the Jubilee clips securing the vacuum pipes to the air filters.

Three flat-bladed screws secure the distributor cap which is also removed along with all 12 plug leads. At this point the rotor arm is also removed for safety.

Dismantling the cross-pipes from the carburettors.

The engine was then securely mounted on a specially-made stand which enabled Dave to strip it of ancillaries and carry out a detailed inspection. This stand allows the engine to swivel through 180 degrees and has its own drip-tray for the odd amount of fluid that may not have drained out before.

Easing off the air bleed pipes, removing the main balance pipe from its hose connection, duplicated on the other side of the engine, the whole pipe assembly can be lifted clear of the engine.

The next stage was to remove the carburettors complete with water rails. Twenty ½in bolts need undoing per side, the outer bolts also securing the four engine lifting points as well.

The two air filters were removed, held on by four 9/16 AF bolts each side, each bolt with its own rubber washer which luckily were intact. The filters will be stripped and repainted before reassembly.

Next off came the coil with its base plate and ballast resistor, noting the spacers which must be retained and refitted upon reassembly.

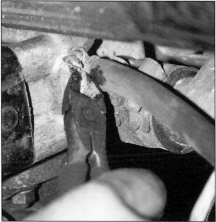

The water bleed hose needs disconnecting to give access to one of the bolts below it.

Removing the front water cross-rail...

...which also means disconnecting the hose from the water pump to the cross-rail.

The bolts through the manifolds carry a special spacer to take up space normally occupied by fuel injection equipment on American spec models.

The heater return pipe is also removed held on via a flexible hose and Jubilee clips and is also attached to the sump via a bolt.

First view of engine internals shows a crystaline action between the water (and/or anti-freeze) with the alloy which will need to be cleaned out.

After undoing the bolt securing the oil dipstick holder, allowing same to be removed, all the manifold holes into the engine are 'bunged' to prevent ingress of foreign bodies.

At the rear of each cylinder head 5/8in banjo bolts are undone, allowing the oil pipes to be disconnected. There was no need to retain the special copper washers as these will be replaced upon reassembly.

The 3/4in banjo bolt on the side of the engine was also undone, again aiding removal of the oil pipes.

The core plugs were starting to decompose, so these will all be replaced later.

Still on the oil feed pipes, after disconnecting the wire to the oil gauge and light sender, the camshaft oil feed pipe assembly can then be totally removed.

There is still lots to do on stripping down the engine, more of which will be covered in the next article, starting with the removal of the throttle pedestal.

With careful teasing the manifolds can then be withdrawn from the engine, taking great care that nothing drops through the holes into the engine.

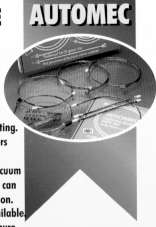

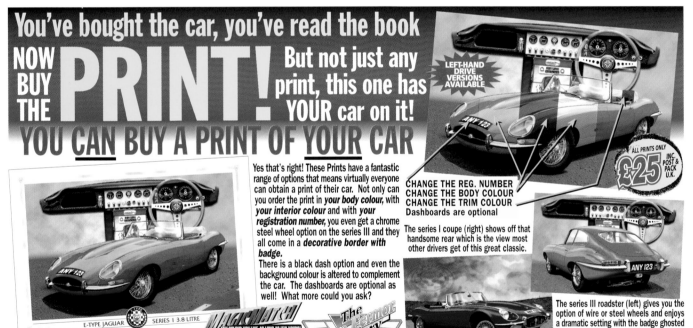

THE HERITAGE LINE

PART 8

By Nigel Thorley

JAGUAR-DAIMLER HERITAGE TRUST "E" TYPE REFURBISHMENT

Nigel Thorley continues with Dave Marks' stripdown of the engine from the Jaguar-Daimler Heritage Trust "E" Type.

Work continued with the removal of the throttle pedestal. This and other items involved in the stripdown are shown here in picture format.

Four 7/16" AF bolts secure the pedestal to the "V" of the cylinder head.

Once lifted clear, the pedestal reveals a gasket for reuse and in this case a hole in the head (later cars had this blanked off).

With the pedestal removed Dave put the gasket back with the bolts for safe keeping and blanked off the hole to prevent ingress of water or foreign matter.

Three bolts secure the distributor in place which need an Allen key to remove. Each bolt should be undone a few turns at a time.

Next off was the water pump elbow held on by three 1/2" AF bolts.

The distributor can then be lifted clear of the engine again revealing a hole in the head which needs blanking off.

Once removed with the aid of a soft faced mallet, the extent of water corrosion be seen.

The power steering pump was removed by undoing the two 9/16" AF bolts and locknuts and by its tensioner which is secured to the base of the water pump.

With all holes in the head blanked off to prevent ingress of foreign matter, Dave's attentions turned to the front of the engine.

The water pump was then removed which revealed again the extent of corrosion.

The front two-part pulley removal commenced with the undoing of the two long 1/2" AF bolts, two of which also hold on the 7/8" AF extension (used to turn the engine over in service).

A

B

C

Above – photos, A, B and C. To get the rear pulley off a pulley-lock is attached to prevent it moving while a 5/16" AF nut is undone.

Next the cone attached to the front of the crankshaft nose is removed with the aid of a Woodruff key. This cone should be checked because they are prone to cracking.

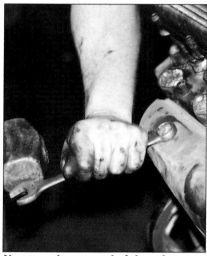

Next was the removal of the exhaust manifolds, starting with the heat shields held in place by 3/4" AF bolts and spring clips that secure same to the base of the manifolds.

Each of the four exhaust manifolds are held on by six 1/2" AF nuts.

With the manifolds removed, further water ingress was noted in the exhaust ports, possibly a sign of a head gasket blowing. Further investigation will be required in due course.

Dave next removed the combined oil cooler and filter housing held on by 1/2" AF bolts, care being taken not to strip the threads.

The oil cooler removed revealed basically good condition except for the known problem of thin oil.

However, Dave was still concerned by the corrosion in the coolant.

Next month Dave will finish off the engine stripdown of the V12 engine.

Next off came the sump pan held on by no fewer than 32 1/2" AF bolts!

THE HERITAGE LINE

PART 9

By Nigel Thorley

JAGUAR-DAIMLER HERITAGE TRUST "E" TYPE REFURBISHMENT

Nigel Thorley continues the report on Dave Mark's stripdown of the Jaguar Daimler Heritage Trust Series 3 "E" Type rebuild project.

With the numerous sump bolts removed, the lower interior of the engine can be viewed which looks in reasonable condition.

Six 7/16in nuts hold the sump baffle plate in position which was then removed to reveal.....

...the extent of sludge build up in the sump which indicates the general state of the unit. This will be thoroughly cleaned before refitment of course.

Removing the 1/2in AF bolts then allows the timing cover to be completely removed from the engine.

A large 7/8in Whitworth nut must be removed, allowing the pipe to the oil filter housing to be removed.

The power steering to engine bracket has to come off held on by one 5/8in bolt.

It is then necessary to extract the studs from the base of the timing case. Strictly speaking it is normal to remove to head to extract the timing case but with care the studs can be removed eliminating this necessity.

At this stage the stripdown was finished as far as Dave Marks was concerned as Tony O'Keeffe of the JDHT was able to get the engine checked over and rebuilt back at Whitley where many of the new parts would be made available for the engine rebuild. It may be possible at a later stage to report on their work although this is being handled by the JDHT mechanics in between many other activities involved with their collection of vehicles.

When the engine is built and tested, it will be returned to Dave Marks for installation into the shell once more.

In the meantime Dave Marks has, at this time, sent away the many ancilliary items for powder coating and the many new parts required for the brake, suspension rebuild are being collated. We will therefore recommence, in a couple of issues, with Dave's build-up of the rear independent suspension assembly.

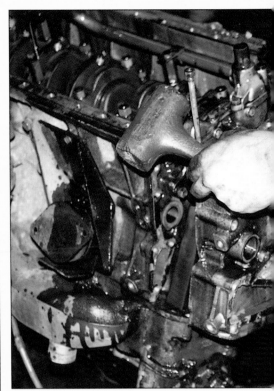

Gentle persuasion with a soft-headed mallet was required to remove the timing case.

In the meantime the bodyshell has been with Renascence Cars in Atherstone where we initially covered their stripdown and part repair. As many will have seen from the N.E.C. Classic Car Show in Novemeber, the shell is now finished and painted. We will report back on their work next in this "E" Type Series 3 project, after which the shell will be temporarily stored back at Jaguar awaiting the installation of mechanicals by David Marks.

The general state of the timing gear was not bad at all in relation to many other aspects of the engine identified during this stripdown.

THE HERITAGE LINE

PART 10

By Nigel Thorley

JAGUAR-DAIMLER HERITAGE TRUST "E" TYPE REFURBISHMENT

This month Dave Marks takes a rest as the V12 engine is returned to Jaguar for their specialist rebuild treatment at Whitley (more on this later) and the bodyshell gets its finishing touches in the careful hands of Tom Priestnall of Renascence Cars.

Very little in new panelwork was required for the "E" Type; here a new front closing panel was fitted to the offside, the nearside still in perfect condition.

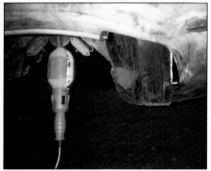

Some corrosion around the wheel-arches was addressed by cutting out the bad metal and welding in new steel.....

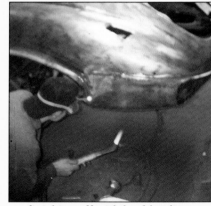

.....finishing off with lead loading.

All repaired areas were polyestered while the rest of the good bodywork was taken down to bare metal.

It was eventually decided to fit brand new doors as one certainly required a new skin, the other slightly less remedial work. In view of the overall condition and requirements by Jaguar it was felt best to fit the new panels instead.
The completed shell was blocked down completely and then coated with a yellow epoxy primer which adhered too the metal like an etch-primer.

Sealer was applied to other vulnerable areas to prevent ingress of water in future.

This is followed by the normal grey undercoat primer. Bear in mind that the panels you see attached here were actually removed during the primer coating to ensure all edges, etc. were fully covered.

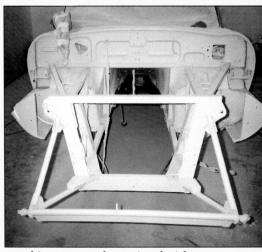

.....this area was then primed with the rest of the car.

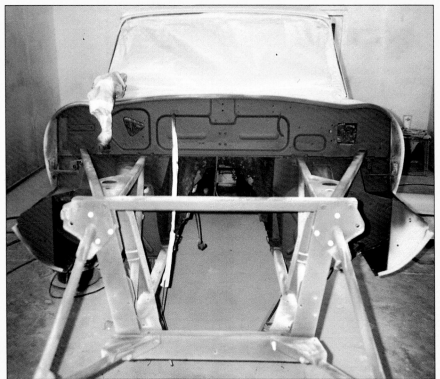

The vulnerable under-rear floor area and sill edges were treated with a flat stone chip

Because of some rust in the metal bulkhead, the area was treated with Finnigans No.1 rust-proofer.

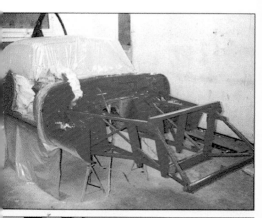

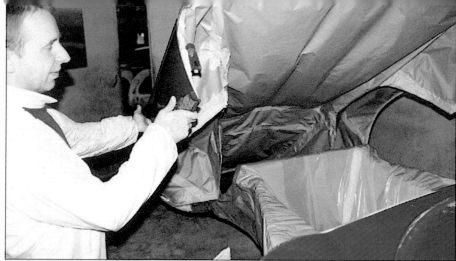

Renascence attention to detail in fully masking off the interior of the bonnet to ensure no overspray from the final paint finish.

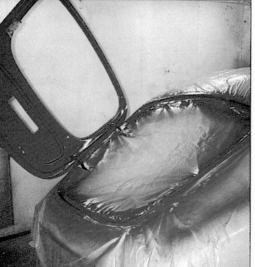

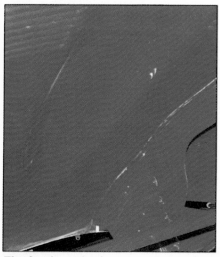

The final touch, the superbly-finished underbonnet area of the Heritage "E" Type.

Top coats were firstly applied to the engine compartment/bulkhead and even rear tailgate interior with the main bodywork masked off to protect against overspray. When thoroughly finished these areas were then masked up and the exterior bodywork prepared for colour.

The finished shell polished and on display at the N.E.C. Classic Car Show last November.

No rest for the wicked as Renascence staff put the finishing touches to the display including a backdrop of photographs of the restoration to date.) The finished product received a total of three top coats of two pack paint, three grey primer coats, two epoxy coats and three polyester coats

Full colour application to the exterior bodywork followed, the final finish being left for several days to fully harden off.

THE HERITAGE LINE

PART 11

JAGUAR-DAIMLER HERITAGE TRUST "E" TYPE REFURBISHMENT

Nigel Thorley brings us up todate with the latest on the Jaguar-Daimler Heritage Trust ex-road test 'E' Type Series 3 fixed head coupe.

Renascence have been working hard on the body-work of the 'E' Type and had most of the work finished for the N.E.C Classic Car Show last November. Allowance

was made for the paint to harden sufficiently before trim was refitted, Jaguar also provided some new chromework and other items that were necessary to finish off the job.

The body, now finished and built up, has been temporarily returned to Jaguar's Whitley plant for storage whilst Dave Marks gets back to the mechanical aspects of the running gear (which will be reported on later).

The engine has now been rebuilt by John Jacob, a Jaguar man from Whitley, who found most aspects in remarkably good condition despite the tell-tales first identified on stripdown. This is wrapped up on a pallet again awaiting return to Dave Marks for refitting at a later date.

The following pictures show how well the car looks now:-

John Jacob of Jaguar proudly shows of his work on the 'E' Type V12 engine.

The front frames and under-bonnet area.

The completely rebuilt 'E' Type engine with new alternator and other ancillaries ready for refitment to the bodyshell.

Has anyone got a correct fuel gauge they would like to donate to the JDHT? The one from the car has been missing for a numbe of years apparently.

Renascence have done a wonderful job with the paintwork.

Detailing to the inner rear wheelarch will help protect the car in future use with the Trust.

The interior has been replaced as was so there is still some detail finishing to be carried out.

THE HERITAGE LINE

PART 12

The return to the work in refurbishing the Jaguar Daimler Heritage Trust ex-press car, "E" Type Series 3 fixed head coupe.

The story so far...

The last time we reported on the Heritage "E" Type, the V12 engine had been rebuilt by Jaguar themselves at Whitley, as had the differential. The finished body and paint work (carried out by Renascence of Atherstone) had also been completed, with the bodyshell stored back at Jaguar awaiting the refitment of mechanics by Dave Marks.

Since that time the stripped components of the subframe and other underbody items had been sent away for powder coating, cadmium plating etc as required, and the new parts had been gathered in readiness.

For the resumption of this story, Dave Marks starts with the detailed build-up of the independent rear suspension.

Rear Hub Bearings

His first task was to put the new bearings into the rear hubs.

The various components (minus calipers) that make up the rear subframe of the Heritage "E" Type.

One of the cleaned rear hubs and the component parts that make up the hub bearings – Set of rear wheel bearings comprising 2 taper roller bearings plus 2 seals, and the trunion bearing kit also comprising 2 taper bearings plus 2 felt seals, locking rings and seal covers.

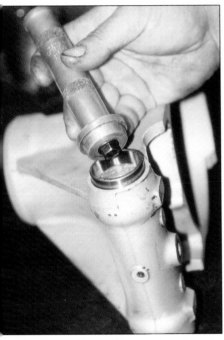

Starting with the fulcrum bearings, the first job was to insert the new race, a relatively tight fit, and here Dave uses a professional drift, ensuring an even load to push the race in cleanly and flush with the hub.

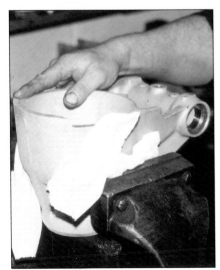

For the next part Dave secured the hub in a vice, note the use of cushioning to prevent damage to the hub.

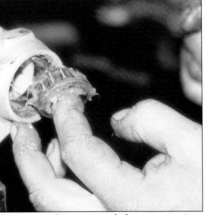

Greasing the race and the appropriate bearing. The latter is inserted as shown.

With the main fulcrum pin inserted and a combination of spacers and shims, an old fulcrum nut (so as not to damage the Nyloc thread on a new one) is temporarily screwed in place. Once in position, it is possible to feel any play in the pin, which must be eliminated.

The play is eliminated by removing the appropriate number of shims and in most cases this can be done by 'feel'.

However, the professional way is to measure the pre-load with the aid of a dial gauge using the workshop manual measurements.

For an example of how this is achieved, with a dial gauge in position, let us say an excess movement is measured at 5 thou; if you were to take 6 to 7 thou worth of shims off that, you would end up with a pre-load of 1 to 2 thou.

In this case, the correct bearing adjustment recommended by Jaguar is 1 thou pre-load.

With the dial gauge set up, magnetically attached to the vice for solidity, by forcing the pin in both directions and taking two readings on the dial gauge, this registered 6 thou of movement. Dave then had to take 7 thou in shims off to get the correct end-float.

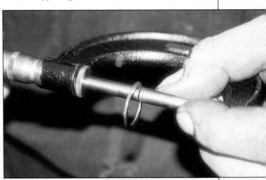

Measuring the shims with a micrometer enabled Dave to get the measurement correct first time.

The next task was to insert the main rear wheel bearing. There are two different sizes and it is impossible to fit them incorrectly. The race is fitted first and again pressured in, here with Dave using his professional drift to ensure an even spread. The change in the 'ring' of hammer will indicate when the race is fully fitted.

The second race is again drift fitted from the inside of the hub. This picture shows both races fitted, looking down into the hub.

Next came the fitting of the bearings, again two different sizes and not interchangeable. Adequate greasing is required before fitting.

Next comes the fitment of the bearing seal, a metal seal with a rubber lip. The picture clearly shows the correct way of fitting. The seal is tapped into the hub and must rest flush with the rim of the hub casing.

Next came the extraction of the old outer bearing from the hub, and here Dave uses his trusty hydraulic press. This certainly saves a lot of time and aggro. If you don't have one, it is strongly recommended that you ask a garage to help you out on this job.

With the bearing extracted, the hub is cleaned up ready to accept the new bearing which is also set by shim adjustment. On the end of the half-shaft that goes through onto the splines, shims are fitted to adjust the play as necessary. This aspect will be dealt with later by Dave when fitted up on the car.

The two parts of the hub are driven together via the outer bearing.

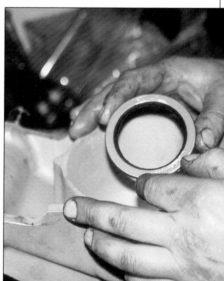

The rear lip seal was then fitted, again driven into the hub.

One of the finished hubs.

Next month Dave Marks continues work on the rear suspension.

THE HERITAGE LINE

PART 13

Dave Marks continues the rebuild work on the Jaguar Daimler Heritage Trust Series 3 "E" Type. Report by Nigel Thorley.

Rear Suspension Work Continues

Now to the lower wishbones and replacement of the inner fulcrum bearings. The old ones had been left in place deliberately during the powder coating process to avoid the inner surfaces getting coated. These were now removed by being drifted out. The inner surfaces were thoroughly cleaned before fitting new bearings.

A good tip that Dave recommends is to apply the grease gun to the nipples and force out the old grease BEFORE fitting the new bearings. This ensures that only new grease will find its way onto the bearings.

The rear subframe cage was also powder coated which meant that the holes to receive the outer fulcrum pins would need filing out to remove the powder coating. The same was required for the lower shock absorber pin mounting points.

It was time to extract the radius arm bushes, the old ones also left in place during the powder coating work. Dave's trusty hydraulic press made light work of this.

Dave normally recommends that new

There are two bearings per arm and of course four arms per wishbone. All interchange. When inserting, ensure the writing on the bearing faces out and that the bearings are driven in to rest flush with the top of the arm. If you are not going to fit up the wishbones to the suspension at the same time it is advisable to protect the new bearings by wrapping them in paper and tape to avoid ingress of dirt or dust.

bushes are inserted with the horizontal line turned 90 degrees; this helps to reduce any tendency to rear wheel steer. *(See picture above).*

Handbrake Assembly

The first job was to assemble the ratchet mechanism by passing the ratchet screw through the spring retainer. The other end of the spring hooks onto the pin which protrudes through the side of the actuating arm. The next stage is to pass the actuating arm over the fulcrum block of the inner caliper half and then manoeuvre the return spring and the cover plate between the arm and the caliper was then attaching the pin to the cross bar inside

As this car is the property of the Trust and is intended to represent the model when new, the bushes were inserted as originally recommended by the factory. As these radius arms get older and old bushes are extracted several times, it is not unusual to find the metal stretches slightly, which, at worst, can allow the bushes to come loose. Dave therefore uses Loctite which sets sufficiently within 15 minutes, totally within 24 hours.

the actuating arm.

The next stage was to insert the ratchet into its clip and pass these over the top of the hollow block inside the actuating arm, then carefully insert the adjusting screw through the other half of the caliper and gently screw in a few threads into the ratchet block. Before affixing the outer cover apply an amount of copper grease to prevent seizure.

Note; the pads only go in one way, in order to follow the curvature of the disc, so that if the caliper is held in position to fit onto the main caliper, the shortest flat of the pads is closest to you and the longer edge runs away.

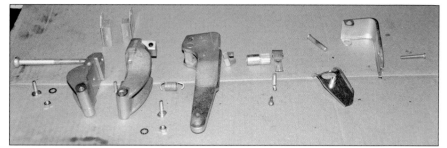

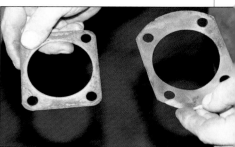

The assembly is made up of two halves of the caliper, the actuating arm, cover plates, the adjustment pin, ratchet device and its locating bracket, tension spring, screws, plus the handbrake pads.

There are two different types of shims, one between discs and diff, the other between discs and half shafts, which Dave kept in the order they were removed from the axle (very important). The combination of the correct number of shims each side will provide the correct degree of camber, but in order to initially shim for the correct caliper to disc relationship, the number of disc to diff shims maybe increased or decreased and subsequently the number of disc to halfshaft shims would then be decreased or increased accordingly.

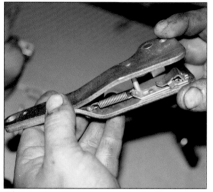

The spring is asymmetrical; the more uniform curve goes through the pin at the base and the hook passes over the bar.

Turning the assembly the right way up, the pads are then inserted. The pads are held in place by slotted head bolts. The bolts must not be over-tightened in case the glue de-bonds between pad and backing plate.

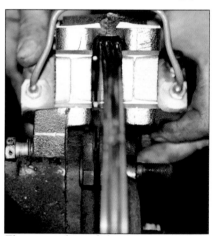

The centre line of the disc must follow the centre line of the caliper, and if it is offset too far in or off the line, the number of shims must be changed accordingly. Dave recommends cleaning the discs with a preparatory cleaner before fitting.

The outer cover has to be fitted, which involves clipping it over the actuating arm, then lining up the holes in the cover with the holes in the actuating arm and the fulcrum block, and passing the fulcrum pin through the lot. A small split pin is then passed through the other end of the fulcrum pin to retain it. Finally a countersunk flat bladed screw passes through a hole in the outer case and screws into the base of the inner cover.

Dave finds that 1.25mm fencing wire is very near to the original used by Jaguar, being niether too brittle nor too soft.

Rear Subframe Assembly

It was then time to reassemble all the parts into the rear axle and suspension subframe assembly. Procedure is to start by fitting the discs to the differential, followed by the calipers.

Fitting the correct number of shims to the differential; the discs were bolted up tight against the diff with the aid of spacers and nuts. This ensures that the discs are in what will be their permanently fitted position. Then the calipers were bolted on and the position of the discs in relation to the caliper noted.

New calipers were supplied by Jaguar and were in fact the type as fitted to a late model XJS V12, the only differences being in the type of piston used and the fact that these later types will be more readily available for a longer period than the originals (no longer available direct from Jaguar). The calipers were bolted directly to the differential casing and then wire-locked.

There is even an art in the fixing of lock wire as Dave explained. Passing the wire through the bolt/nut to be lock wired, a couple of loose twists were firstly made. Then, using mole grips on both twisted ends, carry on twisting whilst exerting

The brass retraction plate, which has a spring-loaded effect to assist the withdrawal of the pads from the disc, must be replaced whenever handbrake pads are replaced. Engaging the two tongues into the slots provided, fit the lock tab and two bolts (with copper grease) and tighten them up. Do not over-tighten as this will make them more difficult to replace at a later date. Easing up the lock-tabs completes the job.

The split pin which locks the screw adjustment must be refitted, preferably from the underside, which will make it easier to access in future in situ on the car.

The completed diff unit with discs and calipers ready for assembly into the cage.

gentle pressure on the wire. The wire should not be stretched too tightly or undue pressure will be exerted over a period which may break it.

The next task was to fit up the handbrake calipers into position. The mounting bracket slots onto the recess on top of the caliper itself. The adjustment pin was kept slack, giving provision for manoeuvring the retraction plate and caliper arms themselves to line up the holes for the pins.

The bolts were then also lock-wired into position. Because these bolts are so important the lock-wiring must be carried out with the twists in the right direction against the tendency for the bolts to undo.

Adjusting the correct gap on the pads to disc should be gauged by a 2mm feeler gauge. In practical terms Dave suggests you lock up the pads hard onto the disc, release the screws back until there is no resistance on the disc; this will ensure the discs are free when the handbrake is not in use and allows plenty of grip when the handbrake is applied.

Caging In

Now work started in earnest on reassembling the diff and suspension into the newly powder coated cage. With the completed diff/discs/calipers ready the cage was pulled over from the pinion end of the diff, a relatively tight fit with the discs and calipers in place but much easier than fitting up the diff first and then the calipers and discs afterwards.

Four top bolts were fitted through the cage and into the differential casing. These are special bolts, coned to give an accurate location for the differential. Each one was fitted but not screwed down tight until all four were located correctly. Then each bolt in turn was removed and Loctited and finally all four were torqued down to 75lbs/ft, each bolt in turn tightened diagonally across rather than in random.

Dave then fitted new brake pads to the calipers; here Dave, unusually, does not recommend greasing the slides as this will allow dust and dirt to collect which can actually hamper the easy removal of the pads. The pad securing pins are fitted in opposite directions, top from the inside out, bottom from the outside in.

The cage could now be inverted to start work on assembly from underneath.

Dave fitted up the carriers to the differential with the two different sized bolts, but not tightened. Then, inserting the large carrier pins through the front of the cage, through the carriers out the other side of the cage, the 'assembly' was ready for shimming.

With the correct shims fitted, the fulcrum pins were removed and the carriers bolted up, torqued to 75 lbs/ft. These

The special shims between the carriers and differential are shaped so they can be inserted without removing the carrier bolts, but should be inserted so that the open end of each shim faces towards the centre of the diff (then, if the worst happens they cannot drop out at a later stage). Invariably the bolts will work loose, due to the torque exerted during the life of the car, allowing the shims to move.

Re-inserting the fulcrum pins; they pass through each wishbone end assembly, comprising of thrust washer, outer seal retainer, seal, inner washer and, finally, the bearing bush, which passes through the fulcrum bearings.

There is one bearing bush for each wishbone arm, but there is a thrust, washer, seal retainer etc, on each side of each arm (8 in total). The cover tube through which the pin passes as it enters and leaves the carrier should not be forgotten. The pins have to be drifted through carefully so as not to dislodge any of the washers and seals, and it can be a tricky job to get right first time. It can be made easier by using dummy shafts – two people familiar with the procedure can do it without. It is a good idea to have another person helping and watching while you drift the pins through. When applying the new nuts at either end they should not be tightened fully until the other pin, bushes and washers on the other side of the diff have been fitted.

were also Loctited and wire locked.

Next to fit were the half shafts, remembering to offer up the correct number of shims to the discs as removed during disassembly. In this instance the existing uni-

At this point Dave recommends applying grease to the nipples to ensure that no seals are dislodged before progressing further.

versal joints were used, as they were in good condition. It is, however, recommended that you always check for free play to avoid unnecessary work in dismantling later.

The half shafts are held onto the output shafts of the differential by means of metal lock nuts. Nylok nuts are unsuitable, due to the heat generated from the differential and brakes, which could melt the Nylok and allow the nuts to work lose. The nuts are 11/16in AF and torqued to 55lbs/ft.

The cage was now ready to accept springs and shock absorbers – which will be treated in the next article.

Dust covers are also refitted, only on the outer UJs on "E" Types, subsequently on all four UJs on later models. The two halves of each dust cover are riveted in position. The side of the dust cover with the hole is meant to accommodate the rubber bung to allow access for greasing the UV joint in situ.

Fitting up the base plate to the cage (which is reversible). Eight 5/16in AF bolts with spring washers pass through the plate into the carriers, whilst three 5/16in bolts and Nylok nuts to the front and rear hold the plate to the cage.

THE HERITAGE LINE

Nigel Thorley continues the story of the IRS rebuild on the Jaguar Daimler Heritage Trust ex-press Series 3 "E" Type. All work carried out by David Marks Garage in Nottingham.

PART 14

We left Part 13 with the assembly of the new rear brakes and diff into the cage. This issue Dave tackles the final assembly and refitting of the cage back into the car.

Before fitting up the cage to the car, the now-repainted bodyshell was manoeuvred onto Dave's hydraulic ramp for ease of access. We will not cover this aspect in detail, as most individuals carrying out such major work on "E" Type suspension will have the car on the ground supported on axle stands. It is, however, worth mentioning that if you have an empty "E" Type bodyshell you must take great care that, once the rear cage is refitted the balance is not upset, causing the shell to tip rearwards, inevitably causing damage. In Dave's case he anchored the front of the car to the ramp to prevent this.

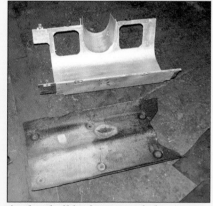

As the shell had previously been completely stripped for painting, the rear heat shield needed refitting before the cage could be assembled onto the car. Quite flimsy, these damage easily and are likely to be well soiled, but with a brush, some cleaner and a bit of aluminium paint, it's marvellous what can be achieved, as you see here.

The shield is secured to the underside of the shell by four self tappers at the front and four spring clips at the rear.

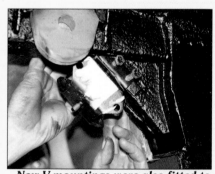

New V mountings were also fitted to the car, each held on by two 5/16in AF nuts and bolts; bump stops were also automatically replaced.

Shock Absorber/Spring Assemblies

Moving back now to the subframe itself, the next stage was to fit the new Koni Classic shock absorbers to the rear springs and refit into the cage. Konis were chosen as they give a good firm ride – and because the original spec Jaguar shockers are no longer available anyway. If the new shock absorbers have been lying on their side in storage, Dave suggests they are 'primed', working them by hand a couple of times to release the fluid as, under normal conditions, the car will not allow the shockers to deflect fully.

Detail Work on the Braking System

Next the handbrake compensator is refitted, held to the cage by two 1/2in AF bolts into captive threads and clevis pins to hold them in place.

The road springs need to be compressed to insert the shock absorbers and it the importance of using a professional approach to this job with a more than adequate spring compressor cannot be stressed too much. Once compressed, the new shock absorbers are inserted. The retaining ring is copper greased and inserted over the shocker and rests under the spring while the collets are fitted. The springs are then decompressed and the unit is ready to fit into the cage.

As new brake pipes are being fitted to the car, Dave had to make up two small lengths to meet a T-piece, both of which are secured to the exterior of the cage by simple clips. Kunifer pipe is being used throughout and as usual this is bought in lengths to be cut and flared as required. (We will cover the whole aspect of making up your own piping and flaring in a future separate article to this rebuild.)

The spring/shock absorber units are inserted into the cage from the underside and are held at the top by a 5/8in AF headed bolt and 11/16in AF nut. Initially these are not tightened fully.

The Koni Classics already have fitted bushes to the exact shank diameter for the Jaguar, eliminating the necessity, with conventional Jaguar shockers, to transfer the sleeve from the old to new units.

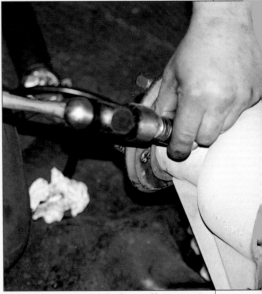

Two things remain before offering up the completed cage to the car. Firstly, to grease the hub bearings and insert the sealing caps. These MUST be pressed in with the aid of an appropriately sized socket and gently hammered in. Otherwise they will 'spread' and either fall out or allow ingress of dirt which will inevitably cause later problems.

With the cage supported underneath the differential casing, the wishbone is moved in its arc, the bottom of the shock absorber is lined up with the appropriate hole, and the fulcrum pin is inserted (after being copper greased). This is not tightened up fully as the pin will need removing later to fit the radius arms. However, now the spring/shock absorber assembly is residing at the correct angle, the top nuts and bolts through the cage CAN be tightened fully.

The last job, arguably the most important and probably sometimes overlooked, is to put fresh oil into the differential!

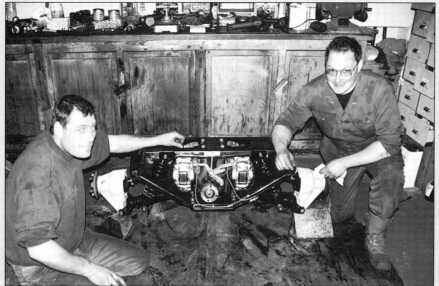

As most readers rarely get the opportunity to see anything of Dave Marks other than his hands, he is here (right of picture) with trusty helper Bob, enjoying the fruits of their labour over the superb sight of a totally rebuilt IRS assembly.

Refitting the IRS to the Bodyshell

As this bodyshell had been completely stripped, the propshaft had been removed. Dave checked the prop for wear in the universal joints, which did not need any remedial work. The shaft is inserted in a tunnel within the floorpan with the splined shaft to the front (engine).

The completed subframe is a substantial and heavy unit which needs careful and balanced manipulation under the car to line up with the V mounts. Two people do help this a lot and it is always best to line up the front mounts first, loosely inserting the nuts until all four are located, then tightening up fully.

Now the shock absorber pin can be reinserted (from front to back of car), not forgetting the spacer between the front shock absorber and fulcrum, used to effectively increase the length of shaft in the wishbone. The pin and the shanked bolt can now be tightened fully, as everything is in the correct angle relationship to the car.

The next task is to fit up the radius arms (which were rebushed in the last article). This involves removing the bottom shock absorber pins (previously loose fitted). The small end of the radius is offered up to the wishbone and a special bolt shanked with one side cut-away to allow it to pass by the wishbone is inserted (copper greased as they are prone to seizing) along with the a spring washer and a lock washer, inserted from the inside out. This is not fully tightened at this stage.

Next the wheel bearings are torqued up to 110lb/ft taking the nut round to the first castellation inserting a split pin.

Checking the End Float

A simplistic way of checking the deflection of the hub is to rock the rear wheel to check for the necessary 1 to 3 thou of end float. However, Dave prefers to use the scientific method which means attaching a dial gauge to the hub to measure the deflection more accurately.

The dial gauge measures in increments of 1/2 thou, changes made by amending the thickness of the brass shim washer at the shoulder of the shaft. Increasing the thickness of the spacer reduces the end float and vice versa.

The shim which allows adjustment on the end float of the rear hub.

With the wheels back on the car, it is possible to fit up the front radius arm mountings to the bodyshell. It will be necessary to locate a bottle jack under the rear hub to supply sufficient 'lift' to line up the arm with its mounting point. New bolts are used throughout, copper greased and first passing through the separate tie-strap, then the bush.

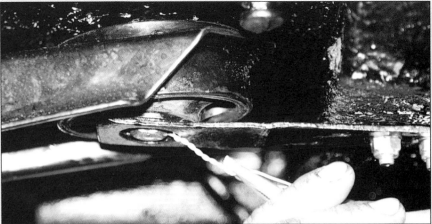

The radius arm mounting bolt is then fully tightened and finally lock-wired into position for safety.

A final check on end float with the wheels attached.

Two new 1/2in AF nuts and bolts are used to secure the tie-strap to the floorpan, inserted from the inside of the car, the nuts tightened from underneath.

The final job would normally be to re-align the propshaft to the output flange of the differential. However, as the engine and gearbox have not yet been fitted to the "E" Type, this will be left to a later date.

THE HERITAGE LINE

PART 15

As Dave Marks reinstates the ongoing refurbishment of the Jaguar Daimler Heritage Trust's "E" Type Series III, this month Nigel Thorley covers the building up of the front subframe.

Work is now back on with the "E" Type and it is time to build up the front subframe using new parts.

Assembling the Top Wishbone

This shows the components for building up one side of the suspension and brake assembly.

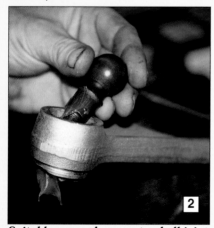

1

Inserting the fulcrum pin into the top wishbone (although this can't be set up properly until it is back in situ on the car).

3

Inserting the ball joint cup with the bevel facing down to the ball...

5

...and then shims. Up to four were fitted to this car. The procedure here is to fit as many shims as necessary until the ball is too tight to move in its cup, then remove one shim.

2

Suitably greased, a new top ball joint is inserted into the wishbone with its rubber collar fitted.

6

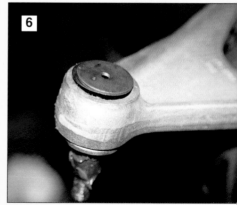

When the correct number of shims is determined the cap can be fitted...

4

...followed by a spring...

..which is held in position with a circlip (the use of the hydraulic press has aided its fitment). It is vital to ensure the circlip seats correctly otherwise the ball joint may 'pop'.

Ensuring the ball still moves freely, a plastic washer and a new grease nipple are screwed into position.

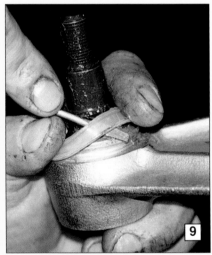

A plastic gaiter retaining ring is pressed over the ball joint and onto the wishbone...

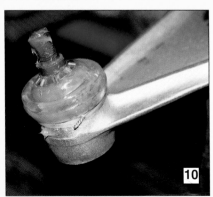

..followed by the gaiter, which is forced into position, suitably greased, over the retaining ring, and lock-wired into the groove provided.

The top wishbone bush is pushed into its housing. This is a hand operation without the need for excess pressure.

Bottom Wishbone

Next, attention is drawn to the bottom wishbone, and a range of components is shown here ready for assembly. The method of construction is different and easier to set on Series 3 cars than the earlier Series 1 and 2 "E" Types.

The lower fulcrum pin and the spacer tube are passed through the wishbone components. Note here that the lower shock absorber pin is inserted through the front of the wishbone (right of picture) with the shock absorber spacing tube.

Ride height adjustment is provided by special bolts with an offset centre over which the cam passes. Note the insertion of the cam between the washer and wishbone on assembly, retained with a Nylok nut.

The next task was to insert the lower ball joint onto the upright. New sealed-for-life units were used, which merely pass through the hole in the upright (without the need for shims) and are secured by thread locked bolts as seen here.

Inserting the bottom wishbone rubber into its housing. Here, again, a hydraulic press has been used, although this is not vital. However, it is vital to ensure that the bush goes in cleanly and squarely.

The brake disc dust shield has now been assembled onto the upright, complete with the steering arm as shown here; a very simple operation, and the bottom separate section of the shield is secured both to the top shield and, via a saddle-clamp, to the upright, held on with 7/16in AF lock nuts and washers.

Inserting the two bearing races into the front hub, one from either side, these are tapped down into position. The rear seal is then gently drifted into position.

Suitably greased, the rear bearing is inserted followed by the rear hub seal which is tapped in flush with the top of the hub.

Moving now to the actual car, the first job in assembly is to insert the lower wishbone arm, with its bushes and brackets, onto the A frame. Note that the insides of the bushes are copper greased, as well as the inner washers on either end of the fulcrum pin. The bolts screw directly into captive nuts welded to the frame.

Fitting the top wishbone arm is very similar. Note that, with the new bushes, it may be difficult to locate all four bolts, so by temporarily doing up the bottom nuts tightly you will, in effect, allow the top ones to draw into position.

The top wishbones are shimmed, as seen here in the picture and...

Next came the assembly of the new disc onto the hub, and during this stage it is vital to protect the inserted bearing against any ingress of dust or dirt. The hub must also be clean and provide a smooth surface for the disc to rest on. Five 5/8in AF bolts secure the disc onto the hub, torqued to 36ft/lb.

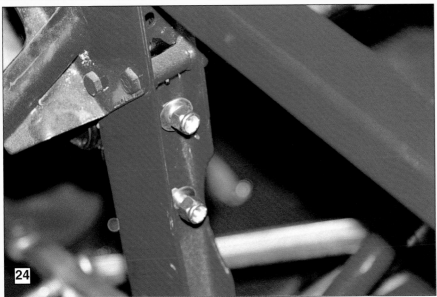

24

...have a washer and locknut inserted from the rear.

25

Once secured to the frame, the two washers are fitted to the fulcrum pin (the smaller last) and new Nyloc nuts are put on loosely, merely to secure the unit together at this stage.

26

The next job was to fit the torsion bar to the body and wishbone. Dependent on chassis number, dimensions for fitment vary. The basic principle is to hang an appropriate bar (made to the exact dimensions required) over the lower shock absorber mounting pin and the top shock absorber mounting pin temporarily secured in position. For this particular car, that vital measurement was 19.525in (hole centre to hole centre).

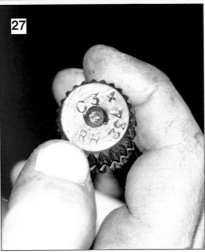

27

The torsion bar itself is simply a piece of pre-stressed steel rod marked left and right hand. In this case the markings are still seen but many times these are obliterated with age, so it is vital, when dismantling, to mark from which side they came.

28

The rear splined end of the torsion bar is passed through a bracket which is secured to the bodywork mid point with two 5/8in AF bolts. Prior to fitting it is strongly suggested that the splines at each end of the torsion bar are thoroughly cleaned so they mesh easily, otherwise it is possible that torsion bar and wishbone may well end up being damaged irreparably.

29

The front splined end of the torison bar fits into the lower wishbone mounting. The relationship of the lower wishbone splined socket to the rear mounting socket is pre-determined by the spacer bar fitted between the top and bottom shock absorber mounting pins, the bottom shock absorber mounting pin being part of the lower wishbone mounting arm. The pitch of the splines on the front and rear of the torsion bar are different and this will allow for a fine vernier adjustment.

Therefore, gently turning the torsion bar one spline at a time from the rear will ultimately allow the splines to engage at the front as well. It is vital not to force the bar at any time to avoid spline damage, this should not be necessary if the splines are thoroughly clean. Once the torsion bar is located gently drift it through until the midway groove on the splined section matches up with the hole in the wishbone allowing the fitment of a grub screw. The fitment of this screw is to control the lateral positioning of the torsion bar. (This picture was taken prior to dismantling).

30

Once the torsion bar is located, gently drift it through till the mid-way groove on the splined section mates with the hole in the wishbone, allowing the fitment of a grub-screw. The fitment of this grub-screw is to confirm the lateral positioning of the torsion bar.

Next Installment
Next time Dave will finish off the front suspension, so the shell will be mobile, awaiting the fitment of the engine and gearbox assembly.

THE HERITAGE LINE

PART 16

Nigel Thorley reports on Dave Marks' return to action on the Jaguar Daimler Heritage Trust's 'E' Type.

It has been some time (February 1998 actually) since we last reported on the refurbishment of the JDHT 'E' Type. A combination of pressure of work with Dave Marks (who has been working on the project for us) and awaiting parts, has meant that the car has lain dormant since that time. However, things are moving apace as the project actually nears completion. So, this month we recommence the story, which will be finished within the next few months in readiness for the official handover to the JDHT.

The Story So Far

For the benefit of new members or for those who have forgotten about the project, a brief resume of the story behind the car is perhaps called for.

The 'E' Type, finished in Regency Red with black interior has been in Jaguar's possession from new. It is quite a renowned car, in that it was extensively used as a press car and was also used for some development work. Over the years the car was left around the factory unused and slowly deteriorated to the point where a major refurbishment was needed. As the JDHT only had one other example of the Series 3 'E' Type (the last roadster made), it was obvious that WHP 205J would be an ideal car to add to the fleet.

So the work was entrusted to Dave Marks, who, along with the Club, sponsored the work which to date has amounted to:

Bodywork – Stripdown the old paint, repair minor corrosion on main shell and bonnet. Replace door skins, some minor outer panels and completely respray to original colour scheme. Wax injection and underbody protection.

Interior Trim – All removed for bodywork repairs and repainting. Seats recovered by Jaguar in-house. Other trim refitted.

Exterior Trim – Mostly intact with some new items, including rear lights and some chrome (Wheels and tyres not yet addressed).

Mechanical – Engine/gearbox removed as a unit. Stripped for inspection by Dave Marks and rebuilt by Jaguar in-house. Rear suspension stripped and completely rebuilt with new parts. Front suspension also completely stripped and rebuilt with new parts.

At the report last February Dave was building up the front subframe and finished off with the refitment of the torsion bar. This month he finishes off the front subframe.

Work Recommences

After the fitment of the torsion bar it was time to fit the new shock absorbers. Koni classics were used. First the bottom of the shock absorber is located on the lower wishbone with a washer and a castelated nut.

It is necessary to jack up the bottom wishbone at this point to align the securing bolt of the shock absorber to the top mounting, again with appropriate washer.

The principle of jacking up the wishbone also enables the bottom ball joint to be located, carrying the upright, passing it through the hole in the wishbone, fitting the washer and a Nyloc nut.

The top ball joint is next, which also locates into position at the top of the upright.

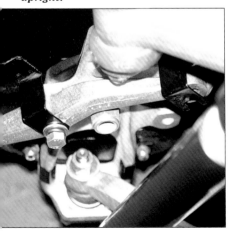

Next comes the stub axle, and here, whilst it makes no difference, convention from Jaguar is to fit this with the flat at the horizontal position facing upwards. Tap it into position with the washer over the back and and 1in AF nut which is torqued to 107 lbs ft.

The main brake disc shield is held in place loosely at this stage by a bolt through the steering arm as the brake calipers will be fitted in a later article.

The hub bearing is greased at this point and fitted to the hub as it is bolted onto the stub axle.

After refitting the large washer and castelated nut, this is tightened to locate the bearings firmly, and is then slackened off until the whole hub spins freely with excess free play. The castelated nut is then gradually tightened, again to bring the bearing up to a measured amount of free play judged by feel. Once this free play was correctly ascertained, it was then split pinned for safety and the grease cover replaced to prevent the ingress of dirt and dust. A new grease nipple was also fitted but the hubs will be set up more accurately when the car is finished.

The finished front assembly.

Steering rack

The rack itself was in good condition so was merely cleaned up and new bushes, gaiters etc fitted.

The locating brackets are held on by two studs integral to the bracket with 5/16in AF nuts and one 5/16in AF nut and bolt

Before fitting the rack, the anti-roll bar is located back onto the car. This consists of the bar itself and two bottom brackets that also carry horns, rubber bushes and two drop arms.

The bushes are wrapped around the anti-roll bar as shown.

The anti roll bar with its new bracket and horn extension is fitted (two nut and bolts although there are four holes) with the split in the bush facing towards the front of the car.

For the fitting of the drop arms, the nuts and bolts were copper-greased, which insert from the outside in with washers on the inside and outside. The lower 5/8in bolt passes through the lower wishbone.

The two rack mounts are bolted directly onto the steering rack via three nuts and bolts as previously explained. Then the rack is offered up to the front of the car. From the back of each mount a single threaded stud passes through the frame and bolts up tight to it. The two other bolts locating each rack mount are essentially safety bolts, whereby they pass through the outer plate of the steering rack mounting, and then by means of a spacer bolt up tightly to the main back plate of the mount. This provides for positive location of the steering rack mounts to the frame of the car, and yet allow a safety device in case the rubber between the inner and outer faces of the rack mount should split, then the spaced out shank of the extended bolt passing through the front face of the bracket will prevent the rack from moving excessively.

The purpose of the sandwich of two pieces of metal with a rubber insert is to provide a degree of protection again back lash of the steering column and rack rattle.

The rack is offered up to the steering column universal joint to get the location correct.

Finally the track rod ends are located into the steering arms and tightened with a flat washer and 3/4in AF Nyloc nuts (observant readers will note that in this photograph these track rod ends are not new as at this stage - the car merely needed to be made mobile and were subsequently exchanged).

With the front wheels back on the car the vehicle was now mobile again and ready for the next stage, starting next month with the preparation for the engine/gearbox refit.

The completion of the Heritage Series 3 E-Type

The principle behind all of the work carried out on the Heritage E-Type was to refurbish rather than to restore. Although as a press car it had suffered a pretty hard life, the originality of the car and the fit of the panels was good. It would therefore have been a pity to completely rebuild the bodywork and end up with a show car too good to use on the road.

Apart from the necessary replacement items, much of the trim was refitted as removed, particularly because some of this trim had already been restored by Jaguar some years ago. Some re-chroming was necessary and various rubbers were replaced.

An important aspect of the refitting was to follow the photos taken during the strip down to ensure correct alignment of pipes, position of warning labels etc. Most of the these photos figure in the episodes shown in this book and will serve as guide to other Series 3 restorers, especially those who are not starting with a completely assembled vehicle.

After various test drives to check out the car, minor adjustments to fit, finish and running were made (often a neglected exercise when owners are too eager to get their beloved cars back on the road). Then, of course, there was the obligatory MoT, which the Heritage E-Type passed with flying colours.

Finally, a lengthy drive of a couple of hundred miles was undertaken to ensure that the car behaved well in all conditions. It then underwent a thorough valet before being handed back to Tony O'Keefe, curator of the vehicles at the Daimler Heritage Trust Museum in Coventry.

The E-Type has now returned to its home and will remain an important part of the Trust's display of historic Jaguars. And not just as a static exhibit - it is planned that it will be regularly used and shown at historic events, making it an excellent ambassador of Jaguar's heritage.

Nigel Thorley